SAUCES

Edible

Series Editor: Andrew F. Smith

EDIBLE is a revolutionary series of books dedicated to food and drink that explores the rich history of cuisine. Each book reveals the global history and culture of one type of food or beverage.

Already published

Apple Erika Janik *Barbecue* Jonathan Deutsch and Megan J. Elias *Beef* Lorna Piatti-Farnell *Beer* Gavin D. Smith *Brandy* Becky Sue Epstein *Bread* William Rubel *Cake* Nicola Humble *Caviar* Nichola Fletcher *Champagne* Becky Sue Epstein *Cheese* Andrew Dalby *Chocolate* Sarah Moss and Alexander Badenoch *Cocktails* Joseph M. Carlin *Curry* Colleen Taylor Sen *Dates* Nawal Nasrallah *Eggs* Diane Toops *Figs* David C. Sutton *Game* Paula Young Lee *Gin* Lesley Jacobs Solmonson *Hamburger* Andrew F. Smith *Herbs* Gary Allen *Hot Dog* Bruce Kraig *Ice Cream* Laura B. Weiss *Lemon* Toby Sonneman *Lobster* Elisabeth Townsend *Milk* Hannah Velten *Mushroom* Cynthia D. Bertelsen *Nuts* Ken Albala *Offal* Nina Edwards *Olive* Fabrizia Lanza *Oranges* Clarissa Hyman *Pancake* Ken Albala *Pie* Janet Clarkson *Pineapple* Kaori O' Connor *Pizza* Carol Helstosky *Pork* Katharine M. Rogers *Potato* Andrew F. Smith *Rice* Renee Marton *Rum* Richard Foss *Salmon* Nicolaas Mink *Sandwich* Bee Wilson *Sauces* Maryann Tebben *Soup* Janet Clarkson *Spices* Fred Czarra *Tea* Helen Saberi *Whiskey* Kevin R. Kosar *Wine* Marc Millon

Sauces

A Global History

Maryann Tebben

REAKTION BOOKS

For Noah and Ethan

Published by Reaktion Books Ltd
33 Great Sutton Street
London EC1V 0DX, UK
www.reaktionbooks.co.uk

First published 2014

Printed and bound in China
by Toppan Printing Co. Ltd

A catalogue record for this book is available
from the British Library

ISBN 978 1 78023 351 2

Contents

Introduction

My own sauce history follows a circuitous path, marked by blind stumbles into sauce revelations. A confirmed omnivore since childhood, I have always been pro-sauce, but I had no idea how limited my experience was until I landed in France during a year of study abroad. When I watched a French friend make vinaigrette by measuring oil, vinegar and mustard into a salad bowl before adding the greens, I realized that 'salad dressing' for her was not the array of colourful sauces in plastic bottles that I had in mind. When I ordered crêpes at a crêperie, the server asked if I wanted the '*supplément Chantilly*', but the words were meaningless to me. My blank look prompted her to fetch a sample for the table and we were delighted to find fluffy, vanilla-scented whipped cream in the cup. Since then, I've never eaten a dessert crêpe without it. In France I learned that language can be a barrier to understanding sauce, and that sauce often requires experience and context. I learned that for some sauces, a little goes a long way, even if you have purchased a kilogram container of mustard in a moment of weakness from the Grey Poupon shop in Dijon and wonder how you'll ever get to the bottom.

Once my sauce curiosity was piqued, I found sauces everywhere, but they remained mysterious. Kraft Macaroni

Crème Chantilly (vanilla whipped cream).

and Cheese sauce seemed foolproof until I saw someone stir the butter into the hot macaroni until it was absorbed, then add the milk and cheese powder. The sauce was grainy and dry. It dawned on me that all of the elements had to work together to make the sauce; at that moment I realized that even Kraft could teach cooks how to *monter* ('finish') a sauce with butter. I took the trouble to make sauce for Steak Diane with shallots, wine and mustard and was astonished that it tasted exactly like A-1 Steak Sauce. A Vietnamese friend helped me understand that fish sauce can smell terrible and still taste delicious. I have never understood the appeal of hot fudge on cold ice cream, but I was captivated by a caramel-bacon dessert sauce I encountered in a restaurant. The chef had been invited to contribute a dessert to an all-bacon menu for a James Beard Foundation dinner. The exquisite result taught me that sauces are a venue for culinary creativity even though they belong to a long rule-bound tradition. This book explores all of these elements of sauce: the linguistic challenges, the French standards, the global reach of sauce, the emphasis on rules and the openness to novelty that sauce allows.

The opening chapter will examine the origin of sauce in its ancient forms: fish sauces in Asia that coexisted with Greek *garum* and Roman *liquamen*, medieval sauces redolent with spices, and elemental vinegar and mustard. These foundational sauces, used independently and as essential ingredients in a variety of prepared sauces, enhanced food in a direct and vital way. Vinegar links ancient and modern sauces. It is still used for practical reasons (vinegar's acetic acid content kills bacteria and makes food safer to eat) and because its flavour has become canonical. Even with modern methods of food preservation in place, vinegar remains central to sauce because we have come to appreciate its bracing flavour. Condiment sauces in particular imitate their complex, sharp, spicy and pungent ancestors. The focus of the second chapter, condiment sauces stand between found-ational sauces like soy and *garum* and the main-dish sauces that envelop a piece of meat or fish, merging old flavours with modern techniques. Although tomato ketchup is usually the prime suspect in arguments about the homogenization of global cuisine, condiment sauces have distinct national identities. The third chapter follows the evolution of medieval sauces through the golden age of sauce in France, defined by the use of butter and the advent of flour liaisons for thickening sauces, from seventeenth-century practitioners

'Britain's Best': O.K. Sauce advertisement, 1952.

through Carême and Escoffier to the post-nouvelle cuisine era. Meat sauces of every sort are the subject of the fourth chapter, featuring British gravies and 'gravy' for pasta as two sides of the same coin. Sauces that fit none of the previous categories or that merit special examination, such as oddly named sauces and the sauces of molecular gastronomy, are included in the fifth chapter. The final chapter attempts to reconcile national sauces with the traditions and culinary preferences of their country of origin and to consider the 'master sauces' that cross continental divides.

I

The Origin and
Conception of Sauce

Love could be called a sauce, able to give flavour to all foods.
Bénigne Poissenot (1583)

A book on the history of sauces must first confront the challenge of defining a sauce. It is easy enough to find examples of
specific sauces codified by famous chefs (béchamel, espagnole)
or by commercial ubiquity (tomato ketchup, brown sauce), but
in the abstract it is difficult to establish a sure definition. A sauce
is usually liquid (soy sauce, Worcestershire) but not always
(jellied cranberry sauce, hard sauce) and can fall somewhere
between liquid and solid (salsa, mustard). It is often made from
meat or made to accompany meat (gravy, *ragù bolognese*) but can
just as easily be vegetarian or intended for vegetables (vinaigrette, mayonnaise). And sauce occupies every level of cuisine
from high (sauce financière with truffles) to home (roast beef
with gravy) to low (ketchup on a fast-food hamburger). A
history of sauce must also consider the language used to
describe or name specific sauces, as well as that used for the
generic term or concept of 'sauce'. Across languages, sauce
terms change and develop depending on the specific use of
the sauce and the food traditions of the receiving country. The

etymology of 'gravy' from Old French through British English to American-Italian English is one pertinent example, as are the homonym sauces: Indonesian *kecap* (or *ke-tsiap*) is not the same sauce as British or American ketchup; German mustard is not the same as Italian *mostarda*. Even within a single language, the nomenclature for sauce can be remarkable. In French, 'coulis', 'jus' and 'sauce' are all general terms for sauce, to say nothing of the tree of named French sauces.

However, as this book will demonstrate, sauces of all kinds have certain core attributes. For the purposes of this book, sauces are taken to be food accompaniments, usually in a smooth liquid form, that are applied to a dish in order to enhance its flavour. Sauces are not ingredients but occupy a complementary role. Dressings, gravies and dips are all sauces because they are refined preparations (as distinct from raw materials) served with a dish but distinct from it. Syrups, spice pastes, oils, vinegar and even salt complement food but do not fit the definition of sauces because they are elemental ingredients. Some sauces are condiments – ketchup and mustard, for example – but not all condiments are sauces, since some are more solid than liquid or can be eaten on their own, such as pickles and relishes. There are admittedly some grey areas (is sour cream a sauce? is caramel?) and it would be impossible to include every sauce in this book. In its broadest definition, sauce is a food enhancer, sometimes complementary and sometimes purposely counteractive; it is not a main dish and is never essential to eating. It bridges consumption and decoration on the plate; it is edible but it does not stand alone. Finally, sauce is unnecessary, but cuisine would be unthinkable without sauce, and sauces are everywhere. Sauce is attractive as a subject of culinary attention because it allows for wide creativity and adaptation to available ingredients, tastes and traditions. The dominant sauces of a national cuisine are closely tied to the foods available in that region, but they are also informed by cultural forces: vegetarianism in Japan displaced fish sauce for soy sauce, anti-Catholicism made Britain a country of gravy, and rapid industrial growth in the u.s. encouraged ready-made, shelf-stable ketchup and condiment sauces.

Viewed historically, sauce has evolved considerably in ingredients, application and philosophy (the purpose of sauce). Early techniques used fermentation to produce savoury, long-lasting sauces that were sometimes combined with sharp or fragrant spices. The guiding principle was balance: these sauces aligned flavours and were believed to mediate potential health risks. The quantity of spices that characterized ancient and medieval sauces was not meant to disguise putrid meat – this is a longstanding myth that has been debunked – but to keep foods in balance with bodily humours, following dietetic rules developed by ancient physicians. Sauces served this purpose well, combining a number of components at once to address the qualities of the main ingredient. For this reason, ancient sauces nearly always functioned as condiments and were never 'integral' sauces cooked with the main dish or from its drippings.

Pottery jug or sauceboat, from ancient Greece, 2800–2300 BC.

Soy sauce fermentation in pots with bamboo lids, at a small factory in China, 1919.

The concept of gravy for meat required several centuries of development and a significant reconsideration of the role of sauce. Sauces of the late Middle Ages and the early modern period, heavily spiced or not, began to leave behind medical considerations in the interest of flavour. There was a gradual but noticeable shift in sauce philosophy from counteractive to complementary that remains today, with certain notable exceptions. In the eighteenth and nineteenth centuries, especially in Europe, main-dish sauces tended to cover food and to merge with it. The industrial age heralded changes to sauce ingredients and sauce preparation in the domestic kitchen, with home cooking on the decline and main-dish sauces becoming special occasion fare. After the changes brought by nouvelle cuisine, classically trained restaurant chefs aimed for simplicity in sauces made from the natural juices of cooked meat and little else. More recently, modernist cuisine has recomplicated sauce with new forms and techniques.

How Soy Became Sauce

Although they were more paste than liquid, some of the earliest named sauces were the savoury condiments of ancient China called *chiang*, a general term for sauce, paste or fermented or pickled foods. *Hai*, one version of *chiang*, may have been made by fermenting salted, dried strips of meat in wine. In *Lun Yu* (or *Analects*, *c.* 465 BC), Confucius wrote that he would not eat food without its proper *chiang*, meaning a 'liquid or colloidal condiment containing bits of finely digested meat or other edible products'.[1] After soybeans replaced meat in these condiments late in the first century BC, *chiang* came to mean fermented soybean paste. Soy *chiang* was the dominant flavouring condiment in China from the third century until the seventeenth century, replaced by soy sauce (*chiang yu*) in the mid-eighteenth century, although the term *chiang yu* was in use as early as the twelfth century to designate the liquid derived from *chiang*. Soy sauce is also called *chhing chiang* or 'clarified *chiang*' in more elegant registers; it is, in essence, named 'sauce'.

The term *chiang yu* (or *shih yu* in Southern China) expanded the meaning of the word *yu*, which formerly referred to an oil or an oily liquid extracted from a solid. The liquid from fermented soybeans did not look like an oil, despite the name, and the word *yu* came to mean 'sauce' in this context. The grammatical example of *chiang yu* (soy sauce) gave rise to other sauce names in Chinese, including *hsia yu* (shrimp sauce) in the eighteenth century and the more recent *hao yu* (oyster sauce; *hor yao* in Cantonese), neither one denoting an oil but a flavouring sauce.[2] A preference for liquid condiments over semi-solid pastes emerged in the seventeenth century in China and coincided with a shift to soy-based condiments from those made from meat. Soy sauce is now the principal flavouring sauce in Chinese cooking and is used both as a condiment on its own and an ingredient in other dishes. The only remaining animal-based *yu* product is Chinese fish sauce, named *yü lu* or 'fish dew', a product of more recent origin.

Japanese *shoyu* (soy sauce) was likely adapted from Chinese methods in the fifteenth century, when the word first appears in the Japanese language. The eleventh-century *Tale of Genji* included references to *miso* and *hishio* (meat and fish sauces) used as condiments at court banquets, and another soy sauce named *tamari* became popular beginning in the fourteenth century. *Tamari* and *shoyu* are close cousins and are prepared nearly identically, except that *shoyu* contains wheat and *tamari* normally does not. The vegetable-based soy sauce may have gained popularity in Japan at the same time as Buddhism and its vegetarian diet did, another influence from China. *Shoyu* added flavour and colour to the traditional Japanese diet of fish, rice and vegetables; it was also believed to increase appetite and promote digestion. Dutch traders with Japan introduced 'India Soy' (as the sauce was known in English) to

Earthenware jugs used for the sale of soy sauce in England, 1800–1830.

Wooden kegs of Kikkoman soy sauce bound with bamboo braids, used to export Kikkoman sauce beginning in the late 19th century. Soy sauce was packaged in kegs until 1965.

Westerners in the seventeenth century. The sauce subsequently became a popular condiment for meats in Britain and the British colonies in North America in the eighteenth century, resulting in a vogue for soy sauce cruets in silver frames for elegant table settings. Industrial manufacturers began to export soy sauce regularly to the western u.s. in the late nineteenth century and expanded in the early twentieth century, packaging soy sauce in wooden kegs until the 1960s. The Mogi family of Japan, owners of the major Japanese soy sauce brand Kikkoman, opened a factory in Wisconsin in 1973, heralding a dramatic increase in consumption of soy sauce in the u.s. By the 1980s, Japanese soy sauce consumption per capita had grown to five times that of the Chinese.[3] However, the growing influence of Western cuisine on Asian markets has slowed soy sauce sales in China and Japan in recent years, while sales have increased in the u.s. with the popularity of sushi and other Asian foods.

Fish Sauces

Fish sauce does not play a prominent role in Chinese cuisine but it serves as a foundational sauce in other Southeast Asian culinary traditions. Vietnamese *nuoc mam*, Philippine *patis*, Thai *nam pla*, Indonesian *kecap* and Burmese *ngan-pyaye* are prepared by fermenting fish and siphoning off the resulting liquid. Burmese and Thai fish sauces from salted, fermented whole fish date from at least the twelfth century. The highest quality Thai *nam pla* is made with anchovies, but other fish and even mussels are sometimes used. Whole sea fish are normally used to make Vietnamese *nuoc mam*, although it has become common to use freshwater fish and even shrimp. The use of fish sauces in China and Japan is likely the result of nineteenth-century trade with the more water-centric nations of Southeast Asia, especially Vietnam, known for the superior quality of its fish sauce. *Nuoc mam* production in Vietnam may have preceded that of other Southeast Asian countries and it is certainly home to the most developed fish sauce industry, but since there is a lack of documentary evidence it is unclear when fish sauce was first produced there.

The charmingly named *yü lu* of China gives itself away as a product that came after soy sauce; if the sauce had been produced at the same time as other *chiang* sauces like soy, the organic derivation of the term would be *yü chiang yu* or 'liquid from fish paste'.[4]

One of the core characteristics of these sauces is their meaty or meat-like flavour, best conveyed by the Japanese term *umami*, meaning 'savoury taste' or 'deliciousness'. In areas where rice is a staple and meat consumption is low, the *umami* sauces stand in for meat, even when the meat-like flavour comes from soy, and facilitate the ingestion of a sufficient quantity of rice, the major source of protein. Fish sauces and soy sauces serve identical purposes in these cuisines and the choice of one over the other varies inside countries and in step with economic changes, according to the availability of the main ingredient. Where fish are plentiful, fish sauce predominates; where soybeans grow well or are cheaper, soy products are more prevalent. In Japan and the Philippines soy sauce and fish sauce can be substituted for one another in recipes,[5] and in Indonesia *kecap* is listed as a soy sauce in some sources and a fish sauce in others. Both fish and soy sauces are easy to preserve and have a long shelf life, another factor in their widespread adoption across the region.

The best documented of the ancient fish sauces, *garum*, was dear to the ancient Greeks and adopted by the Romans for use as a flavouring component in sauces, but much remains unclear about its ingredients and its name. The terms *garum* and *liquamen* are intertwined in the evolution of this sauce, often without clear distinctions. Archaeological evidence indicates that *garum* – the liquid drawn from amphorae of fermented, salted fish – was being traded in Greece as early as the fifth century BC and reached the height of its popularity in Rome between the first and third centuries AD. The term *garum* comes from the Greek word *garon* or *garos*, the name of a type of fish, and the *Geoponica*, a Greek agricultural manual written in the sixth century AD, gives a nearly complete recipe for *garum* made from fish intestines and blood. Pliny, writing in his *Natural History* in the first century AD, recorded a description of *garum* made from whole fish that is attributed to Apicius, a renowned gourmand who lived in first-century Rome.[6] The Roman cookbook named for Apicius but likely compiled in the fourth or fifth century AD calls for *liquamen* in most sauce recipes and refers to *garum* only in the form of secondary sauces like *oenogarum*, fish sauce mixed with wine, and *oxygarum*, fish sauce mixed with vinegar.[7] Columella made reference to *liquamen* but not *garum* in his *De re rustica*, a first-century book on Roman agriculture. The terms *garum* and *liquamen* were used interchangeably in the *Geoponica* and other sources to refer to sauces made from whole fish, fish entrails or fish blood. *Liquamen* eventually became a generic term for any fish sauce. More recent scholarship suggests that the term *liquamen* may have been used to impose a Latin word on a sauce with a Greek name. Romans may have adopted *liquamen* as the term for fermented fish sauce made from whole fish and *garum* for the higher-status sauce made from fish blood; *liquamen* is believed to have been an ingredient used by cooks in the kitchen, hence its lower status, and relatively expensive forms of *garum* may have been used by elite diners as a table condiment.[8]

In Roman recipes for sauces made with *garum* or *liquamen*, the fish sauce was mixed with spices, herbs and vinegar as a dipping sauce or a dressing for cooked meat. Pepper, found in every sauce recipe in Apicius, figured prominently in these sauces, as did rue, thyme, lovage and *laser* (an herb similar to

Pottery mortarium for grinding and mixing sauces, Roman Empire, 1st century AD.

asafoetida that was extinct by AD 50), and honey balanced sharp flavours. Whether cooked or used cold, these sauces were prepared using a mortar, first to grind pepper with various seeds and herbs and then to mix this paste with liquid ingredients. Alternatively, the spices and herbs were pounded into a paste and reserved, as pre-made spice pastes are today, then added as needed to *liquamen* or wine for a quick sauce. These pastes were called *hypotrimma* in Greek and *mortaria* in Latin, bearing the name of an essential tool that served as both a grinder and a mixing bowl for sauces in Greek and Roman kitchens.

Over six centuries through the Greek and Roman period, fish sauces evolved and changed names, eventually disappearing in Europe with the disintegration of the Roman Empire. *Garum* has had a renaissance of sorts with modern-day diners who seek the elemental flavour of the ancient sauce, and it is once again available from speciality food shops. M.F.K. Fisher was ahead of her time when she admired the rusticity of *garum* in the late 1940s as an alternative to the 'onslaughts of marshmallow-vegetable-gelatin salads and such which smile at me in Kodachrome from current magazine advertisements'.[9] Her recipe is frank and unsentimental: expose salted fish to the air 'until putrid', then serve.

Sauce Principles

The terminology of ancient sauces helps to explain the role of sauce in the past as well as illuminating our modern vocabulary for sauce. The verb *condire* – literally 'to flavour' – in *Apicius* indicated the addition of a spice mix or finished sauce to a dish. The noun *conditura* meant 'that which will season or flavour' and was occasionally used in recipes to connote a seasoning mix or *ius* (meat juice) for a sauce. The shared root of these words gives us 'condiment', a specific kind of sauce that gives a contrasting flavour to a finished dish, and the Italian verb *condire*, to apply a sauce that complements but does not dominate a plate of pasta. Ancient sauces were clearly separate from the main ingredients of a dish; they were often served separately as dipping sauces and were conceptually separate as a purposeful contrast to the properties of the meat or vegetable with which they were paired. Early Chinese sauces, like the Greek and Roman sauces that would succeed them, aimed to perfect and correct flavours, to put food into proper alignment in a direct way. In a text from the seventh century AD, Yen Shih-Ku declared that as a harmonizer of flavour, '*chiang* [sauce] is to food what a general is to an army.'[10] Greek and Roman cooking of late antiquity took the notion of harmony a step further, applying medical principles from Galen, Hippocrates and others regarding the alignment of bodily humours to sauce/food pairings. Sauces with 'hot' elements, such as pepper or burned bread, could be used to render 'cold' meat such as beef more digestible and therefore more nutritious, and sauces changed according to seasons as well. In winter, hotter foods like ginger and sharp vinegar were required; in summer, spices and wine were avoided in favour of lemon juice and herbs. Cold, moist meats like goose could be balanced with toasted bread and garlic, but chicken (dry and delicate) called for white wine and cider vinegar. Vinegar was technically considered 'cold' but was used constantly as a base for sauces.

In medieval Europe, cooks continued to adapt sauces more or less to dietetic principles. The *peverata* sauce for game in Platina's *De honesta voluptate* (1474) is typical, with toasted bread, pepper, wine and vinegar used as a contrast to crude game meat. The fourteenth-century British cookbook *Forme of Cury* includes a nearly identical recipe for roast venison served with *peverade* sauce (pepper, toasted bread and vinegar). Medieval sauces remained separate from the meat they covered: they rarely included meat juices and were usually poured over already cooked meat. Dietetics manuals, not cookbooks, normally indicated which sauces should be paired with which foods. But the tide began to turn in the late Middle Ages towards considerations of flavour that were sometimes inconsistent with medical principles, and cookbooks began to dedicate separate sections to sauces. The fourteenth-century dietician Maino de' Maineri (or Magninus) of Milan observed in the *Opusculum de saporibus* that flavour and dietetics were not antithetical in sauce. In fact, delicious sauces encouraged digestion and health, although they could be dangerous if they induced diners to overindulge. Sauces had been adapted to meet medical principles, but culinary practice also regularly contradicted medical theory. Platina followed the rules with his *peverata* sauce, for example, but he broke them with recipes for boiled mutton and waterfowl, both 'moist' meats. Magninus made it permissible for flavour to be a guiding principle over dietetics, and French cookbook authors of the period especially took up the cause.

Magninus promoted Camelina sauce, made with the spicy mustard plant, for roast rabbit and chickens; in the late fourteenth century Taillevent in *Le Viandier* paired it with these meats and also kid, lamb, mutton and venison. As the Middle Ages wore on, some elements of ancient cooking fell out of favour on aristocratic tables, including pepper and garlic, thought suitable only for the crude stomachs of peasants. By the sixteenth century direct conflicts began to emerge between cooking practice and medical treatises.

Sauces with mustard seed, pickles and vinegar were specifically condemned by Estienne, a sixteenth-century French medical writer, for example.[11] Yet these sauces continued to be used and promoted in European cookbooks as flavour preferences ultimately outweighed medical concerns.

In the late Renaissance, a shift to complementary sauces accommodated custom and court fashions but ran counter to earlier dietetic standards. The new sauces for meat made from the meat's juices and butter reinforced the meat's inherent qualities, while a medically sound sauce would have corrected the meat with contrasting condiments that minimized its potentially dangerous effect on the body. The butter sauce won by a landslide. By the eighteenth century in Europe, heavily spiced contrastive sauces no longer appealed to diners, and attention to Galenic principles, however half-hearted, had faded away.

Vinegar and Early Mustard

As a flavouring agent, vinegar has been in use in China at least since the age of Confucius. Vinegar figured prominently in ancient sauces and as a preservative for food, and some of these sauces still exist on modern tables. A recipe in *Apicius* for preserving fried fish called for drenching just-cooked fish in hot vinegar.[12] This preparation survives as *escabeche* (called caveach in English cookbooks), a vinegar sauce served at sixteenth-century banquets for Spanish colonizers in Mexico and still prepared in the Yucatán. Mustard also has ancient origins and when combined with vinegar it becomes a base for numerous other sauces. In fact, mustard as a sauce has not undergone much of an evolution since it first appeared. Both Plautus and Pliny made reference to the edible mustard

Nicolas Larmessin, *Vinegar-seller* (*Habit de vinaigrier*), 1695, engraving.

plant (*sinapi* in Latin) and its seeds, and Columella gave a recipe for the condiment in *De re rustica*: pounded mustard seeds mixed with vinegar and ground almonds or pine nuts. The English word 'mustard' and its variants in Romance languages is rooted in 'must', or unfermented grape juice for wine, the acidic liquid that was later used in place of vinegar to create the sauce. Early recipes vacillated between wine, vinegar and verjuice and some added herbs or other flavourings. The prepared sauce became a commodity in medieval Europe, important enough that Etienne Boileau, a government official in Paris in the thirteenth century, accorded the right to make mustard to the *vinaigriers* who sold vinegar and other vinegar-based sauces door-to-door. The fourteenth-century French cookbooks *Le Viandier* and *Le Ménagier de Paris* both included recipes for preparing mustard and recipes with mustard as an ingredient, and the condiment continued to flourish in France through the seventeenth century, when mustard vendors in Dijon formed guilds and dominated the industry. Mustard is an emulsifying agent, making it a popular ingredient in vinaigrettes, and it has preservative qualities that are useful in pickles. With its long and illustrious history, mustard should be the king of condiment sauces (and it came close in France), but victory in that realm goes to the swift and the nimble, those sauces that adapt quickly to changing tastes.

2

Condiment Sauces

The historical uses of the word 'condiment' from the Latin *condire* (to put in, to flavour or to preserve) reveal the elemental nature of condiment sauces and the fluidity of the term's definition. Roman recipes viewed spices as condiments and Cicero used *condimentum* in its most general sense in *De finibus bonorum et malorum* (45 BC): '*Cibi condimentum esse famem*' (literally, 'the best flavouring for food is hunger').[1] In Europe during the Middle Ages and the Renaissance, condiments were a class of ingredients used to make foods dietetically correct. Sauces belonged to this category, as did certain fruits and vegetables. Condiments balanced the bodily humours and the textural qualities of foods, providing a contrast in flavour and in composition. These components were not considered foods by themselves but as partners for other foods, as are all sauces in the broadest sense of the term. Vincenzo Corrado defined sauces precisely this way in *Il cuoco galante* (1773): sauces were 'not foods but condiments' created to season food 'or to revive a listless stomach or else to stimulate the tastebuds of any palate'.[2]

Condiment sauces also gained favour as stable preparations that travelled well, a quality of great importance on ships in the age of European exploration and colonization. In the nineteenth century condiment sauces very often became commercial sauces. Thanks to new technologies devised by Nicolas Appert in 1809 for canning and preserving food, factories could produce on an industrial scale many of the condiments that had previously been made at home. Most of the present-day condiment sauces still provide a contrast in flavour, texture or aesthetics, just as the original condiments did, and they are still viewed as secondary foods: in current industrial parlance, condiments flavour the 'host foods' with which they are served. Condiment sauces allow the diner to customize his or her food to a personal standard, especially in the context of domestic or casual cuisine, in contrast to the chef-controlled plated sauces of haute cuisine.

Ketchup is perhaps the most recognizable American condiment sauce. Andrew F. Smith called it the 'Esperanto of cuisine' and noted that 'few other sauces or condiments have transcended local and national culinary traditions as thoroughly as tomato ketchup.'[3] Tomato ketchup arrived in America via a circuitous route from Asia and the 'India Soy' products imported to Britain from the seventeenth century onwards, as English cooks imitated these fermented sauces with their own preparations. Etymologically the word 'ketchup' may have emerged from the name of the Indonesian sauce *kecap* or *ke-tsiap*, but the sauce has similarities to the vinegar sauce *escabeche* from Moorish Spain, whose name derives from the Arabic word *iskebêy*, meaning vinegar pickle. Vinegar and strong spices, not tomato, connect the fermented origin sauces (soy and fish) to eighteenth-century British ketchups. A recipe for 'English ketchup' in Eliza Smith's *The Compleat Housewife* (1729) gave instructions to boil vinegar and white wine with anchovies, mace, ginger, cloves, pepper and horseradish before it was bottled, corked and aged for a week or more. Like the *umami* sauces from Southeast Asia, English

Geo. Watkins's mushroom ketchup, still available in the UK.

ketchups did not always contain fish. They served primarily as a flavouring for meat or a substitute for meat gravy. These sauces benefited from a long shelf life characteristic of the fermented sauces that preceded them. Elizabeth Raffald promised that her recipe of 1769 for 'Catchup to keep seven years' would survive a trip to the East Indies.[4]

The key to ketchup's popularity in the late nineteenth century was its adaptability, both in terms of ingredients and use. Mushroom and walnut ketchups, with or without anchovies, were popular until early nineteenth-century recipes began to include tomatoes. The British transmitted a taste for fermented ketchups to the American colonies, where recipes for mushroom, walnut and tomato ketchups begin to appear in cookbooks like Richard Alsop's *Universal Receipt Book* (1814) and Mary Randolph's *The Virginia Housewife* (1824). English sources also used various spellings, including 'catchup', 'calchup' and 'catsup', with no change in meaning. William Kitchiner's 'Superlative Catsup' in the American edition of *The Cook's Oracle* (1822) took mushroom ketchup a step further by reducing it twice, at which point he said it should be called 'Double Cat-sup or Dog-sup', a joke that worked less well when the recipe was reproduced word for word by N.K.M. Lee in *The Cook's Own Book* (1832) under the heading 'Mushroom Ketchup'.

Fermented ketchups had fallen out of favour by the early twentieth century in the U.S., but there is still a limited market for walnut and mushroom ketchups in the UK. Like many condiment sauces in the nineteenth century, homemade ketchups were still widespread at the turn of the twentieth century in Britain and the U.S., but are now almost unheard of on the domestic front. Thick tomato ketchups gained favour only in the twentieth century when hamburgers, hot dogs and french fries became widespread finger foods. Present-day commercial ketchups are, by contrast with early varieties, indistinguishable from one another in consistency, ingredients and use. Commercial bottling of ketchup began in earnest in the U.S. in the 1820s, and the Henry J. Heinz company began selling its now famous ketchup in 1876. In the 1980s, the single-serving ketchup packet arrived, as did plastic bottles for ketchup. The flavour of Heinz tomato ketchup, the most popular brand worldwide, is so entrenched in the U.S. that consumers are reluctant to embrace new varieties. Salsa ketchup, introduced in the 1990s, was a notable failure. For all its success with tomato ketchup, Heinz tried and failed to upgrade ketchup with green and purple colouring in 2000. EZ Squirt ketchup was marketed to children, and the line eventually expanded to pink, orange, teal and blue varieties. After a surge of initial interest, the product proved unpopular and

California Home Brand tomato ketchup (here spelled 'catsup') produced in Alameda, California, in the early 20th century. The company merged with Hunt Brothers, another ketchup and condiment producer, in 1946.

The Canadian speciality *poutine* (french fries, gravy and cheese curds).

disappeared from store shelves in 2006. Ketchup appeals to young and old, but it seems that Heinz overestimated parents' willingness to buy a separate bottle of ketchup for the kids. In response to the company's effort to reposition tomato ketchup with these changes, a market analyst advised restraint: 'In a world of spices, ethnic sauces and infinite options, Heinz Tomato Ketchup should remain focused and be the Coke of the sauce world.'[5] Around the world, ketchup has adapted to national flavour profiles with spicy and curry flavours, but in the U.S., plain tomato is the rule.

Pervasive as it may be, ketchup is not the only sauce served with french fries worldwide. British fish and chip shops serve malt vinegar and HP sauce, the French choose mayonnaise or aïoli and the Canadians own *poutine*, an inspired combination of fries, gravy and cheese curds. Belgians, who claim to have invented fries in the seventeenth century, are the undisputed leaders in fry condiment sauces. *Frietkot* stands typically offer fifteen or more sauces, many of them in the mayonnaise family. Among the most popular are ketchup, curry ketchup, *andalouse* (mayonnaise, tomato paste, onion, lemon juice), *américaine* (ketchup and mayonnaise) and *samouraï* (mayonnaise and harissa).

Mayonnaise originated in nineteenth-century French classical cookery but has grown into a global condiment sauce because of its versatility. Still a popular homemade condiment, it can serve as a dip or a spread; with garlic it becomes aïoli, tied to Provence; with red pepper and garlic it becomes a *rouille* for bouillabaisse. Mayonnaise entered the commercial market in the u.s. in 1907 in Philadelphia, where a deli owner sold 'Mrs Schlorer's Mayonnaise' using his wife's recipe.[6] Richard Hellmann began to sell prepared mayonnaise from his own deli in New York in 1912. The product was later marketed as Hellmann's Blue Ribbon Mayonnaise and the company had become the largest industrial mayonnaise producer in the world by 1923. Kraft marketed its jarred mayonnaise in the 1930s and introduced a hybrid mayonnaise/salad dressing called Miracle Whip in 1933. Kewpie mayonnaise, Japan's first commercial mayonnaise, created in 1925, is currently enjoying a spike in popularity outside Japan among foodies who praise its 'super-umami' qualities; its ingredients include egg yolks rather than whole eggs, rice vinegar and MSG. The Empire Mayonnaise Company, founded in Brooklyn in 2011, makes 'luxury mayonnaise' with a constantly rotating list of flavours, black garlic and smoked paprika among them.

At the opposite end of the flavour spectrum from creamy mayonnaise, pungent English condiment sauces share the

Kraft advertisement from the 1939 New York World's Fair.

An entirely new type of salad dressing . . . a delicious combination of mayonnaise and old-fashioned boiled dressing. Tangy, tantalizing, Miracle Whip has a wonderful flavor all its own; is uniquely smooth and creamy.

Miracle Whip Salad Dressing
A NEW KIND OF DRESSING CREATED BY KRAFT

True Mayonnaise of real home-made goodness is now available Kitchen Fresh at your food stores. Ask for Kraft Mayonnaise—a superb blend of choice ingredients including FRESH LEMON JUICE.

KRAFT GENUINE Mayonnaise
Kitchen Fresh

38264

contrastive flavour qualities prized in early versions of ketchup. A recipe for Harvey's sauce made from soy, walnut pickle, anchovies, vinegar and cayenne appeared in London cook Richard Dolby's *The Cook's Dictionary* in 1830, but it was already being sold commercially by the Lazenby firm as 'Harvey's Fish Sauce' in 1815. The Lazenby family claimed to have purchased the recipe from a man named Harvey, and sued other firms who attempted to use the trademarked name.

The debate over whether Harvey's sauce was a generic product like soy or ketchup or a trademark owned by Lazenby's ended in 1870 when a British court opened the commercial right to produce Harvey's sauce to all, as long as it was not called 'original Harvey's sauce' and did not use the Lazenby name.[7]

Created at roughly the same time and with similar ingredients, Worcestershire Sauce has a tentative link to India. In the 1830s Lord Marcus Sandys, the former governor of Bengal, asked the Worcester-based grocer Lea & Perrins to make his favourite Indian sauce from a list of ingredients that he provided, likely a combination of soy, fish and spices. The first batch 'made their eyes water' but when the containers of sauce were set aside and forgotten, age and fermentation tempered the sauce into an appealing condiment.[8] Production began at the factory in Worcester in 1835 and Worcestershire Sauce became so successful that eventually it was exported worldwide,

Lea & Perrins Worcestershire Sauce bottle. The sauce has not changed in nearly 200 years, but the tagline on the bottle has. This version is almost poetic: 'For that instant richness in meat dishes.'

Lazenby's 'Chef' Sauce poster, late 19th century. Note the bottle of Harvey's sauce at bottom left.

even to India. The sauce is now made from vinegar, anchovies, sweeteners including tamarind extract and spices; it is another surprisingly popular fermented fish sauce and the company has never offered a vegetarian version.

Cantonese sauces derived from soy and fish ingredients also belong to the category of 'brown' condiment sauces. Sweet and spicy, hoisin sauce literally means 'seafood sauce' although it does not contain fish; it consists of soybeans, vinegar, sugar and garlic and is often served with roast duck. A Chinese cookbook from 1945 with a preface by Pearl Buck contains the first English-language reference to hoisin sauce (although the sauce is much older), which is called *hoisin cheung* in Cantonese and *haihsien chiang* in Mandarin, another *chiang* sauce relative.[9] Oyster sauce is similarly sweet and pungent, and is made by reducing oysters and soy sauce into a thick liquid. Both hoisin and oyster sauce are now ubiquitous commercial sauces found on supermarket shelves and used in stir fries. A dipping sauce of soy and citrus derived from the Japanese word for vinegar (*su*), ponzu sauce (or *ponzu shoyu*) is served with sashimi and other fish and meat dishes. The word first appeared in the late nineteenth century. Grilled meat with teriyaki sauce, made from soy sauce and *mirin* (sweet rice wine), appeared on restaurant menus in the late nineteenth century in Tokyo, and the first commercial teriyaki sauce was manufactured in 1965 in Hawaii. A similar sweetened soy-based sauce – a mixture of soy, rice wine and sugar – is often used to baste *yakitori* (grilled chicken kebabs).

Fruit-flavoured British condiment sauces may have been inspired by Indian chutneys, as these smooth sauces replicate the ingredients if not the texture of Indian fruit relishes. Popular in the 1850s, Tapp's Sauce was a powerful combination of vinegar, green sliced mangoes, chillies, ginger and garlic, aged for at least a month in the sun. O.K. Sauce, now

HP Sauce in lean times, 1929.

Economical foods can be flavourful

In meat pies, hashes, stews, stocks, soups, sandwiches, and with all cold meat, cheese, bacon or sausages

a little

HP
SAUCE
makes all the difference!

called O.K. Fruity Sauce, was sweeter and contained tomatoes and other fruits; made by Mason's in the 1920s and then Colman's in the 1960s, it has become difficult to find since the 1980s and is now used mainly as a sauce for Chinese take-aways. In the category of 'brown sauce', HP sauce (named for the Houses of Parliament restaurant, where the sauce was rumoured to be served) falls somewhere between thin Worcestershire and thick tomato ketchup but has similar ingredients to Worcestershire, apart from the anchovies. First produced commercially in 1903 in Birmingham and now owned by Heinz, the sauce combines tomatoes with vinegar, dates and tamarind and pairs well with sausages and bacon sandwiches. HP has a rabid following in the UK and in anglophone Canada, where it vies with tomato ketchup as the major condiment sauce for casual dining, despite recent consumer backlash over the company's decision to move production out of the UK and to change to a lower-sodium recipe. The celebrated but fatty English fried breakfast would not be complete without lashings of a sweet-and-sour sauce like HP. The British fervour for these sauces grew out of the tradition of extending the Sunday roast into a week's worth of hashes, sandwiches and cold meat dishes in middle-class homes. Savoury, piquant sauces helpfully enlivened leftover meat, interrupting the monotony and encouraging digestion.

Chop houses in nineteenth-century Britain regularly served mustard with beef and pork, but prepared mustard was established in Europe well before Colman's of Norwich, a flour and starch manufacturer, began to export British mustard around the world in 1830. In France, mustard from Dijon was sold as a prepared sauce by *vinaigriers* from the thirteenth century onwards, and as pastilles to be mixed with vinegar by the consumer by pharmacies in the sixteenth century. The sauce was common enough in France that François Rabelais wrote of pork eaten with mustard in *Pantagruel* (1532) and created a memorable scene in *Gargantua* (1534) of the giant devouring dozens of hams and sausages as his servants shovel mustard into his mouth. Mustard producers in sixteenth-century Tewkesbury, Gloucestershire, shipped portions of prepared mustard paste (to be mixed with vinegar) to London and other commercial centres, and technological innovations in drying mustard seeds led to the production of the first powdered mustard there in 1720. Shakespeare confirmed the city's reputation for mustard in *Henry IV, Part 2* (1597), in which Falstaff calls another character's wit 'as thick as Tewkesbury mustard' (II.iv).

French mustard flourished in Europe in the seventeenth and eighteenth centuries in a profusion of flavours, including vanilla, florals and violet water. In the nineteenth century

British mustard tended to be sharper and spicier, a blend of milder *Sinapis alba* seed and pungent *Brassica* seeds, and it was very often sold as powder, more a spice than a condiment. Prepared mustards were the preferred form in France and western Europe; American and British companies traded in both powdered and 'made' mustard in the late nineteenth century and powdered mustard is still common in the UK. In 1871 the Heinz & Noble Company (Henry J. Heinz's first, short-lived company) added prepared brown mustard to its product line.[10] The most popular American brand today is French's yellow mustard, brightly coloured with turmeric, first sold as 'cream salad mustard' in 1904. British mustards are sharply flavoured to contrast with the roasted or boiled meats they usually accompany; made mustards were sometimes mixed with horseradish to add heat. By comparison, American mustard has a milder flavour, better matched to hot dogs and snack foods like hot pretzels. French mustard ranges from the mild Bordeaux style to Meaux mustard *à l'ancienne* with visible grains, to the eye-wateringly strong Dijon style, sometimes tempered with gentler flavours like tarragon and shallot. Founded in 1853, Grey Poupon (now owned by Kraft) won prizes in 1889 at the Exposition Universelle in Paris for its mustard but was hardly the only successful producer. Paris *moutardiers* Maille and Bornibus challenged Dijon's supremacy in the nineteenth century with truffle, anchovy and tarragon flavours and a delicate Champagne variety for elegant ladies.

Although it is similarly named, Italian *mostarda di fruttà* is quite different from mustard as it is known elsewhere in Europe. Similar to a relish or a chutney, *mostarda di fruttà* is fruit preserved in a spiced syrup, famously produced in Cremona in Emilia-Romagna and usually served with *bollito misto* (boiled meats). It is named for the must or grape juice used in early recipes and shares a lineage with traditional mustard. The recipe for *mostarda* in Martino da Como's fifteenth-century *Libro de arte coquinaria* is nearly identical to Columella's recipe for mustard, calling for soaked mustard seeds to be ground with almonds and mixed with verjuice (the juice of unripe, unfermented grapes) or vinegar. The two recipes for *mostarda* in Cristoforo Messisbugo's *Libro novo* (1557) – one with ground mustard seeds, sugar and spices and the other with vinegar-soaked mustard seeds boiled with apples and vinegar – departed from established mustard recipes but were

Six varieties of mustard, clockwise from top left: white mustard seeds, dry powder, Bavarian sweet, wholegrain French made with black seeds, Dijon-style, American-style yellow.

not fruit relishes. Bartolomeo Scappi's *Opera* (1570) contained recipes for standard mustard (sometimes called 'French mustard' in Italian sources) and 'sweet mustard' (*mostarda amabile*) of grape juice and quince, to which mustard seeds and spices were added.[11] Ippolito Cavalcanti's *mostarda* recipe in his cookbook of 1837 instructed the cook to boil Aglianica grapes '*non con violenza*' until reduced before adding apples, orange rinds, cinnamon, cloves and sugar (but, curiously, not mustard seeds).[12] Dictionary entries for 'mostarda' in the eighteenth and nineteenth centuries hold to the ancient definition of a sauce made from boiled must, mustard seeds and vinegar; *mostarda di Cremona*, the fruit condiment, is a separate, regional confection.

Part of the mustard family and nearly as widespread in world cuisines, horseradish is the foundation of a number of sauces for meats and fish. The Slavic word *chren* for horseradish (*Armoracia rusticana*) pre-dates western European words for the plant, including *raifort* in French and *pepperrot* in Swedish, indicating that the wild horseradish plant originated in Eastern Europe.[13] Crushed and mixed with salt and vinegar, horseradish roots were used medically and for food in Germany by the sixteenth century. British and American cookbooks in the eighteenth century paired horseradish sauces mainly with fish but also with beef and lamb, and horseradish with beef became a staple in nineteenth-century England. The plant was brought to the u.s. by European immigrants, and horseradish mixed with vinegar became a popular homemade condiment in America in the early nineteenth century, especially among English and German immigrants. The 'beef on Weck' sandwich local to Buffalo, New York, owes its signature bun (the salt and caraway seed crusted *Kümmelweck*) and its horseradish topping to German immigrants in the area. In the 1860s Heinz bottled horseradish in clear glass containers to respond to fears of food adulteration, hoping that an emphasis on clean, trustworthy products would convince the public to buy commercial versions of what was normally a homemade condiment.

Tabasco, a vinegar-based hot pepper sauce, was invented in 1868 by Edward Avery McIlhenny in Avery Island, Louisiana, although a similar sauce was served as early as the 1650s in the Mexican state of Tavasco. Trademarked by McIlhenny in 1870, Tabasco sauce is now sold in 110 countries in seven varieties, including green jalapeño and habanero. Tabasco has a global reach but remains American. If there is room for another 'Coke of the sauce world', Tabasco fits the bill in the hot sauce category, since it is served on everything from fast food to cocktails to oysters.

Sriracha sauce, on the other hand, has been called 'the Red Bull' of sauces.[14] It is a thick, hot sauce with garlic, named for a Thai seaport (Si Racha) where the red chilli condiment is well known. Commercial Sriracha (also called 'rooster sauce' for the green rooster on the label) was created in 1980 in California by the Vietnamese founder of Huy Fong Foods. Both Tabasco and Sriracha are widely used as table condiments and both have a loyal following by different demographics. In general, Tabasco is considered the 'grandfather' of hot sauces, while Sriracha is the young upstart. Sriracha is also beginning to stretch its identity: the company claims that their chilli sauce 'has begun to break away from being known as a sauce for only Asian food and now is being known as a hot sauce for all cultures'.[15]

Harissa may be more successful in achieving that goal, given its longer history and steady worldwide expansion. The North African condiment made from hot peppers, garlic, oil and spices shares the heat and the bright colour of Tabasco and Sriracha but has a paste-like consistency. Ubiquitous in

Tabasco pepper sauce in five flavours.

Libya, Tunisia and Algeria, it has spread to Morocco, France and Germany as well as foodie enclaves in the u.s. It serves as a condiment for meats and an ingredient in soups and stews. The sauce probably dates to the Spanish and Portuguese introduction of the chilli to North Africa in the sixteenth century. It shares its name with another North African dish of long-cooked pounded meat and soaked grains, popular in Arab cuisine since the Byzantine era.[16] The two harissas are connected by the mortar traditionally used to prepare each one, and meat harissa (or harisa) is commonly served with spicy harissa sauce.

Mexican salsa has also proven adaptable to multiple contexts as a dip, condiment and ingredient. Like ketchup, with which it has been locked in competition in the u.s. since the 1990s, salsa has been largely reduced to a single commercial form: a chunky sauce of tomatoes, onions, coriander (cilantro) and jalapeños. In Mexico, where *salsa* simply means

Harissa sauce, the spicy, pepper-heavy condiment common in North African cuisine.

'sauce', the fresh tomato condiment is known as *salsa mexicana* or *salsa cruda* (raw sauce), or by the term *pico de gallo*, which is likely a Tex-Mex invention.[17] Other salsas served in Mexico and increasingly in Mexican restaurants elsewhere are made variously with cooked tomatoes, tomatillos and a variety of chillies from mellow serranos to fiery habaneros.

In 1947 Pace Picante sauce was the first commercial salsa sold in the u.s. by Pace Foods of San Antonio. The company introduced a thicker, chunky salsa (the style now associated with the name) in 1988. The label 'salsa' for a range of Mexican sauces, including thin, smooth picante sauce, is important to understanding the announcement in the 1990s that salsa had overtaken ketchup in sales in u.s. markets. Packaged Facts, a market research firm, determined that Mexican sauces as a group (including salsa, enchilada, taco and similar chilli-based sauces) outsold ketchup in 1991, with $640 million in sales to ketchup's $600 million.[18] By 1992, Americans were spending twice as much on Mexican sauces as on ketchup.[19] The news launched a thousand headlines at the time and these stories are still cited as evidence of a cultural shift in America pushed by Latino immigration. But the market research did not isolate sales figures for the thick, chunky sauce most Americans imagine when they hear the term 'salsa'. Furthermore, as critics of this oft-cited claim have noted, ketchup is present in more homes (97 per cent of u.s. households) than salsa (51 per cent).[20] It also costs less per ounce; judged by quantity rather than cost, Americans buy more ketchup than salsa. And yet the metaphorical value of the idea that 'salsa has replaced ketchup' in American culture is significant and enduring, even if the evidence to support the claim is less than definitive. In a book on the formation of the Latino identity in the u.s., Arlene Davila gave 'the "salsa is beating ketchup" phenomenon' as evidence of mainstream acceptance of Latino culture and a challenge to 'the assumption that Hispanic culture is to be used exclusively to market to Hispanics'.[21] In response to his Congressional colleagues' efforts to pass 'English-only' legislation making English the official language of the u.s. in 1995, the delegate from Guam jokingly suggested that America make ketchup the national condiment and warned against the 'non-native' salsa (and soy sauce) invasion.[22] Indeed, commercial salsa has become a mainstream product no longer strictly associated with Mexican foods, and fresh salsas are promoted as healthy, low-fat sauces for many dishes.

3
French Sauces

French sauces belong to a category of their own. They are important because of both their place in haute cuisine and their influence on sauces in other national cuisines. The twentieth-century French chef and food writer Curnonsky claimed that 'sauces are the ornament and the honor of French cuisine; they have helped it obtain and retain its superiority.'[1] No less an expert than Auguste Escoffier declared, 'Sauces represent the fundamental element of cuisine. They have created and maintained the universal dominance of French cuisine.'[2] The classic French sauces that dominate haute cuisine came of age in the nineteenth century, but they grew out of medieval sauces and were shaped by changes in style and technique in the intervening centuries. The French sauce family is a carefully constructed monolith, encompassing everything from vinegar sauces to buttery cream sauces to aromatic jus.

The first step towards the modern French sauce as we know it was the transition from medieval sauces constituted of vinegar or verjuice and spices to sauces made from meat juices and/or fat and thickened with flour. French cooks for the elite in the seventeenth century replaced spices in sauce recipes with what Jean-Robert Pitte calls '*aromates français*' – fresh herbs (especially tarragon, chervil and thyme), shallots, mushrooms, capers and anchovies. With this move, French cooking distinguished itself from other European cuisines. La Varenne's *Le Cuisinier françois* (1651) heralded other important sauce innovations: a *bouquet garni* (or bundle of herbs) to flavour sauces, a *liaison* of flour and fat to thicken sauces (a change from using bread as a thickener) and a preponderance of fat-based (as opposed to acidic) sauces. La Varenne also thickened sauces by reduction, a technique that would become more popular later. The transition to sauces made from a butter-and-flour roux happened gradually, and acid was never entirely eliminated from early modern sauces, although the strong flavour of vinegar was mediated with the addition of stock or oil. Sauces with verjuice or vinegar as a main ingredient remained popular through the eighteenth century and some of these quasi-medieval sauces persist today, such as sauce ravigote (mainly vinegar, herbs and mustard with a bit of oil) and sauce gribiche (a garnish sauce of hard-boiled eggs, vinegar and pickles, served with cold meats, fish and shellfish). Vinegar sauces remain a part of high cuisine, even if they are far from the more modern smooth, buttery sauces, maintaining sauce's legacy from its origins in sharp, fermented preparations. At old-school bistros in France sauce gribiche traditionally accompanies calf's head or brains. In a more modern interpretation, Thomas Keller pairs sauce gribiche with stuffed pig's head and pig's feet at the French Laundry in California, and three-star Michelin chef Yannick Alléno offers 'veau chaud' – a sausage made from calf's head and served like a hot dog with sauce gribiche – at his bistro Le Terroir Parisien in Paris.

The dedication page of La Varenne's *Le Cuisinier françois* called this work 'a treasure-trove of sauces', privileging sauces as the core of French cuisine. Molière echoed this sentiment and the status of La Varenne's book in *La Critique de l'Ecole des femmes* (1663) via the character Dorante, who warned against using theory to judge plays: 'It's just like a man who, thinking a sauce is excellent, wants to determine if it is good according to the principles of the *Cuisinier français*.'[3] And yet La Varenne did not offer a comprehensive chapter of sauces and only a handful of sauces were designated by name: sauce verte (vinegar and green wheat), sauce poivrade (vinegar and pepper) and sauce Robert (verjuice and onion). There were a few meat and mushroom jus with simple recipes, but most of the liquid dressings were called generically 'sauce' or 'ragoût' and were incorporated into the recipe for the dish. Only meat and game sauces were singled out, because a small number of sauces could be served with a large number of roasted meats, and all had a base of some combination of vinegar, verjuice and citrus. The move away from heavily spiced sauces marked a change in the conception of sauce as a cover or antidote for the inherent qualities of the main ingredient; instead, sauce was used intentionally to enhance the flavour of food. This notion was suggested by La Varenne and François Massialot in their instructions on serving roasted meats with sauces that best complement them – the only discussion of sauces as a category by either author.

La Varenne's use of a 'liaison' of fat and flour opened the door to the butter and roux-based sauces that became the foundation of recognizably French modern sauces. A scant 1 per cent of the recipes in Taillevent's fourteenth-century *Le Viandier* contained butter, compared to 55 per cent of all recipes and 80 per cent of sauce recipes in L.S.R.'s *L'Art de bien traiter* (1674).[4] A French sauce without butter is now nearly unthinkable. In *Mastering the Art of French Cooking* (1961), Julia Child noted that the addition of butter at the end of a sauce 'smoothes [it] out, gives it a slight liaison, and imparts that certain French taste which seems to be present in no other

KITCHEN SIEVES (Tamis de Cuisine).

Fig. 141. Fig. 142. Fig. 143.

It is impossible to perform any kitchen work without the use of large and small sieves. Sieves and colanders are indispensable either for straining purées, forcemeats, gravies and broths, for draining purposes or when required to be laid aside for further use.

Tamis for straining sauces, from Charles Ranhofer's *The Epicurean* (1894).

type of cooking.'[5] L.S.R. first called for lard and butter to be cooked 'all of it nearly reddish' before flour and broth were added to create a base for a sauce. Massialot did not adopt the roux wholesale in *Le Cuisinier royal et bourgeois* (1691), but certain sauces, ragoûts and even a mushroom jus called for flour to be added to browned butter or fat and deglazed with liquid.

In seventeenth-century French cookbooks instructions for sauces were usually incorporated into recipes for a specific meat or vegetable dish. But the building blocks for the nineteenth-century master sauces were present in seventeenth-century cookbooks in the form of jus and coulis. Jus (or 'juices') were simply the juices from browned meats, usually extracted with a press. Occasionally the term 'jus' was applied to a reduced broth made from mushrooms or vegetables. Coulis were concentrated liquids made from a base of meat or bones (often ham and veal) and aromatics (onions, clove, thyme, mushrooms), simmered with broth or wine, thickened with toasted bread crusts and strained after cooking. L.S.R.'s cookbook referred to a *coulis universel* that was an early version of sauce espagnole, later to become the 'mother sauce' for all French brown sauces. Not to be confused with the pungent, vinegary brown sauces of English cuisine, brown sauces in French cuisine are prepared with a browned roux and often beef or veal essence, in contrast to the white sauces made with cream or light-coloured stock. Extravagant preparations meant that for elite tables, coulis usually required quantities and types of meat that would have been out of reach of the lower classes. There were a few vegetable-based coulis for lean days, but even these called for status ingredients (truffles, fish stock) and complicated techniques. The word 'coulis' was nearly synonymous with 'sauce' in the seventeenth century but the preparation functioned both as a stand-alone dressing and an ingredient in other sauces. Vinegar-based dressings and early versions of white sauces, by contrast, were always labelled 'sauce'.

The number of coulis expanded dramatically in the seventeenth century. In *Le Cuisinier royal et bourgeois*, Massialot listed 23 different coulis. Later in the eighteenth century, cookbooks aimed at bourgeois households offered recipes for sauces that did not depend on this extravagance. Scaled-down version of sauces derived from court cuisine appeared in cookbooks like Menon's *Le Nouveau traité de cuisine* (1739) and *La Cuisinière bourgeoise* (1746). The latter specifically excluded sauces based on coulis where possible and offered menus with fewer sauces altogether. However, both the espagnole and allemande sauce recipes in Menon's 'bourgeois' cookbook began with coulis simmered with wine and flavourings. In a posthumous edition of 1734, Menon's *Le Nouveau cuisinier* contained only six coulis (veal, white, white for fast days, pheasant, crayfish and crayfish for fast days). Now a term beloved by trendy chefs, a coulis is no longer an extravagant long-simmered base for complicated sauces but usually a purée or reduction of a single ingredient, and fruit coulis are as common as savoury ones. In a reversal of meaning, coulis have become the simplest kind of basic sauce: the French Laundry cookbook reassures home cooks that if the fonds-based sauces are too labour-intensive, glazes and coulis are an effective substitute. In France, *fond* literally means 'base'; fonds are long-simmered, delicately flavoured meat or fish broths.

Eighteenth-century sauces continued to develop the butter-roux profile and introduced new combinations as well: coulis with acid (the post-Varenne sauce Robert), oil or butter with acid (vinaigrette) and egg yolks with acid in an emulsion (hollandaise and related sauces). These innovations led to the development of the other master sauces of French cuisine as well as a string of named and now highly recognizable sauces. The emphasis on sauce was so pervasive at this culinary moment that a new term was coined for a bad cook: *gâte-sauce* or 'sauce spoiler' entered the French language in 1808. The codification of sauce recipes in Marie-Antonin Carême's *Le Cuisinier parisien* (1828) and *L'Art de la cuisine française au XIXe siècle* (1832) grew out of his effort to streamline and simplify sauce preparation, further distancing himself from the coulis in favour of a trio of basic sauces – espagnole, velouté and béchamel – with cold egg-based sauces like mayonnaise treated separately. The simplicity of the system was overshadowed by Carême's fanciful presentations on pedestals draped with ornaments. These sauces are another stage in the transition from contrast sauces heavy with vinegar to discreet sauces of the modern era that added flavour without camouflaging the food being served. The substantial sauces of the pre-nouvelle cuisine Carême era are now disparaged as indigestible and even nonsensical, since they dominated the plate visually and gustatorily, but they are absolutely intelligible in the context of the nineteenth-century explosion of French cuisine.

Carême pioneered the French taxonomy of sauces, a sort of Russian-doll system of foundational sauces that build on one another in a logical way. The old formula for sauce used a base of coulis, added a liaison and the juices from the cooked dish, and finished the sauce with flavourings like onions or verjuice. The new system initiated by Carême combined a coulis (now a glace or reduced stock) with a liaison to make one of the mother sauces (or *sauces capitales*) that was then combined with flavourings to make a secondary sauce. The sauces themselves may not be simple, and the number of possible sauces is dizzying, but the structure is clear. The system is perhaps the reason why French sauces are so entrenched in haute cuisine across the globe: it is comprehensible, logical and adaptable. Louis-Eustache Ude, once part of the cooking staff for Louis xvi, transported French sauce techniques to England in his career in London and in his cookbook *The French Cook; or, the Art of Cookery* (1815). His recipes, even in English, depend on French vocabulary and demonstrate the dominance of French technique on sauce making. For espagnole sauce, for example, the cook must 'let all the glace go to the bottom, and when of a nice red colour, *mouillez* with a few spoonfuls of *consommé* to detach the glace; then pour in the *coulis*.'[6] The book was meant for an English audience, but all of the essential French sauces were represented, including béchamel, Soubise, Robert (onions, espagnole and mustard) and a version of velouté simplified for English cooks who, according to Ude, had fewer assistants and thus required less complicated methods.

Thanks to Carême, an aide-mémoire like the *Répertoire de la cuisine* (an inventory of classic French dishes for professional chefs, the realm of true French sauce making) became both possible and necessary. The *Répertoire* (1914) by Louis Saulnier was a quick reference for thousands of named dishes and preparations, including 176 sauces. It was dedicated to Escoffier but committed to preserving the past and cultivating the present and future of French cuisine. Even for home cooks, the system engenders confidence: Child assured her readers that 'sauces are the splendor and glory of French cooking, yet there is nothing secret or mysterious about making them.'[7] In some ways, Carême's effort to organize and refine French sauces reflected the country's effort to reconstitute itself after the Revolution and subsequent tumultuous political cycles. At least in gastronomy, already an area of French expertise, the nation could lead the way in innovation and accomplishment. Carême hinted at this connection in *Le Maître d'hôtel français* (1822), a rewriting of sorts of French cuisine that attempted to present the splendours of *'la cuisine moderne'* as an evolution of traditional or *'ancienne'* cuisine. Curiously, poivrade, ravigote and Robert sauces endured, sanctioned as modern in their evolved versions. Carême had high hopes for the new era of modern cuisine, positioned at an auspicious moment of artistic and professional advancement, and he noted that the return of the royal family to France (Louis xviii, not long for the throne) would only help the country reach new heights. Carême was less than prescient about the monarchy, but his instincts for cuisine were impeccable.

Once the foundational sauces were named and elevated, new sauces were invented and named, often after historic figures or events. The effort to establish storied histories for these sauces coincided with growing nineteenth-century French nationalism. Some of the sauce legends can be confirmed, but even the invented origins of these sauces illuminate the French history of the period in a compelling way. Many named sauces were simply attributed to an aristocrat or a cook working in his or her service, as with sauce Soubise (created by the chef to the Prince of Soubise) and sauce Béarnaise (invented in a nineteenth-century restaurant and named for

Salmon with sauce Béarnaise, one of the classic white sauces in Carême's sauce system.

Henri IV, a native of Béarne). The French seem to have a legitimate claim to béchamel, but not because of a supposed connection to Louis de Béchamel, a nobleman during the reign of Louis XIV, or his chef. Claims that the sauce (*balsamella* in Italian) was created in fifteenth-century Italy by cooks at Catherine de' Medici's court also seem unlikely. Although Florentine women are known to have used a flour-and-milk concoction called *balsamo* as a beauty mask, the closest culinary mixture of flour, milk and eggs in this period is found in a recipe from Bologna, not for a sauce but a fritter. Similar recipes (from Platina) had reached France before Catherine de' Medici but 'are not the grandparents of béchamel, given the older starch-thickened milk sauces found in France and the milk, bread and egg-thickened dishes in France and England'.[8]

If béchamel is defined as a white sauce with dairy and a roux base, the first béchamel dates to the eighteenth century, since most white sauces before this period are bound with eggs and contain wine, verjuice or vinegar. These emulsified sauces are now part of the mayonnaise family. A recipe in Apicius' *De re coquinaria* for lamb with a sauce of milk and verjuice thickened with wheat may be a distant relative of béchamel, but it pre-dated the use of a roux.[9] The first sauce named béchamel is in Vincent La Chapelle's *The Modern Cook* (1733): it is made with a pinch of flour and cream or milk and cooked until thickened. In two different cookbooks, Menon's version of 'bechameil' was a cream sauce thickened by reduction alone, but a chicken recipe 'à la béchamelle' in *La Cuisinière bourgeoise* had a cream sauce thickened with *beurre manié* (butter mixed with flour). The name béchamel denoted dishes cooked with cream in eighteenth-century works like François Marin's *Les dons de Comus* of 1739 (a sauce with roux and egg yolk) and William Verral's *A Complete System of Cookery* of 1759 (with beurre manié). Not until Carême did béchamel become a foundational sauce from which other sauces could be made. Carême's version began with meat essence and combined a roux-based velouté sauce with cream, an idea he credited to the Marquis de Béchamel.

Mayonnaise is said to have been brought to France in the eighteenth century by the Duc de Richelieu after his victory at Mahon in Spain in 1756, even if the term 'mayonnaise' did not enter the French language until the nineteenth century. Recipes for *sauce froide* in pre-nineteenth-century cookbooks bore a resemblance to what is now called mayonnaise, except that these sauces were not emulsified and had to be kept cold to remain thick. Even Ude's recipe for 'Mayonnaise' in *The French Cook* is a mixture of allemande sauce, aspic and oil that 'must be put to ice'. The sauce of oil and egg yolks that we know as mayonnaise appeared in cookbooks around 1819 and may also have been known as *mahonnaise* or *bayonnaise*. Grimod

Dishes 'à la magnonnaise' (dressed with mayonnaise) from Carême's *Le Cuisinier parisien* (1828).

de la Reynière weighed in on the etymological origin of the word in *Manuel des amphitryons* (1808), dismissing 'mayonnaise' as a non-French word and 'mahonnaise' because it referred to a city of no gastronomic importance (Mahon, Spain). He vouched for 'bayonnaise' because it recalled Bayonne, home of many 'innovative gourmands' and the best hams in Europe. In *The Epicurean* (1894), Charles Ranhofer, who had become chef at Delmonico's restaurant in New York after an apprenticeship in France and positions at two French courts, printed a recipe for 'Mayonnaise Sauce à la Bayonnaise', an egg-based mayonnaise with Bayonne ham and dried Spanish peppers. Carême used another spelling and another etymology: his sauce was called 'magnonnaise', from the verb *manier* (to manipulate or stir), because the only way to achieve this unique creamy, smooth sauce, which is made with no application of heat, is through constant stirring to create an emulsion. Carême offered four versions of *magnonnaise*: *blanche* with egg yolks, tarragon vinegar and olive oil from Aix; *à la ravigote* with chervil, tarragon, burnet and dill; *magnonnaise* made with béchamel; and *sauce provençale* with mustard.

In the twentieth century Escoffier contributed to and reinforced the system of sauce making and naming with his *Le Guide culinaire* (1903), a compendium of thousands of recipes for the professional cook. Under Escoffier, French restaurant kitchens were organized into five *parties* with the *saucier* second in command after the head chef. The sauces in the *Guide culinaire* marked a slight decline in the near universal use of espagnole, béchamel and velouté in favour of aromatic stocks (*fumets*), but the mother sauces still required the building blocks of meat reductions and demi-glace that demanded hours of advance cooking. Escoffier also introduced tomato sauce as the fourth foundational sauce, a significant innovation since Carême. The system pioneered by Carême allowed

Auguste Escoffier (centre left) honoured as Best Chef in France at the Palais d'Orsay, 1928.

Escoffier to multiply the number of sauces while still following the rules by creating new branches of master sauces: from
velouté came velouté of veal, of poultry, of fish and so on.
To these bases could be added a nearly infinite combination
of flavourings, and nearly 300 sauces emerged, all faithful to
Carême's principles.

But the true master sauce in French cuisine and the one
with the most provocative name is sauce espagnole or 'Spanish
sauce'. It is a rich, brown sauce believed to have been named
for the spicy sauces with toasted flour brought to France by
the Spanish cooks that accompanied the Infanta of Spain on
her marriage to Louis xiv in 1660. Massialot's recipe in 1691
for partridge *à l'espagnole* did not call for a roux but rather a
coulis made with roasted partridge and truffles, thickened with
toasted bread, seeming to contradict this genealogy.
Nevertheless, Carême answered those who complained that
'sauce à l'Espagnole' was an affront to French patriotism by
noting that it honoured the Infanta of Spain, wife of Louis
xiv, and that the sauce had been perfected by French
technique and no longer bore any resemblance to the original
Spanish model.[10] By the twentieth century, the sauce
espagnole of roux, veal stock and tomato purée had earned
top billing in Escoffier's 'Grandes sauces de base'.

Sauce allemande or 'German sauce', another foundational sauce of velouté, mushroom or poultry broth, egg yolks
and cream, drew criticism for its name as well. Some
suggested that the designation referred only to the colour of
the sauce – a German blonde sauce as compared to the
brunette Spanish sauce – and not to any national origin.
Carême countered that this sauce had been similarly
improved by French expertise and should be considered
French. In the *Annuaire de la cuisine transcendante* (1874), a writer
named Tavenet widened the argument to include politics,

calling sauce espagnole and sauce allemande primary examples of the weakening of France's national pride and status in the world. He imagined that diners who encountered espagnole and allemande sauces pitied the French for their submissiveness to these nations in an area of supposed French dominance. Tavenet admitted that tradition had its place, but declared forcefully that labelling French products with foreign names was unforgivable. He demanded that 'sauce espagnole' be renamed 'sauce à la française' and that 'sauce allemande' become 'sauce parisienne'. Tavenet was certainly responding to France's defeat in the Franco–Prussian war of 1870-71 and the ongoing French enmity toward Germany following a series of invasions and conflicts. Perhaps bowing to this legacy, Escoffier adopted the change for 'sauce allemande', noting that 'parisienne' was the correct name and that custom alone kept the illogical 'allemande' label. Escoffier claimed that Carême objected to the name 'allemande' as well, although Carême's death in 1833 effectively excused him from the argument. But Carême specified that the only similarity between the French sauce named 'allemande' and German sauce served in Germany was its colour and its consistency. Julia Child opted to call it 'sauce parisienne', 'formerly sauce allemande', but other twentieth-century cookbooks kept the latter name. Espagnole sauce seems never to have been affected by the suggested change. Incidentally, hollandaise sauce, says Pitte, is also 'in reality truly French'.[11]

As much as the 'new modern' sauces in the seventeenth century paved the way for the age of sauce, with innovations made by Carême and the dominance of French cuisine the world over, these sauces did not achieve immediate success outside France. Italians viewed them as suspicious, almost deceptive as a cover for food, even hostile to the stomach.

The butter-enriched, cream-thickened French sauces became even less popular in the first wave of nouvelle cuisine in the eighteenth century, which targeted culinary excess and replaced sauces with jus, and again in the new nouvelle cuisine of the 1960s, which endorsed simplicity and turned away from heavy sauces. Prosper Montagné, later a contributing author to the *Larousse gastronomique*, marked the importance of sauce as a discreet flavouring element rather than a covering for food in *La Grande cuisine illustrée* (1900). One of the ten commandments of nouvelle cuisine in Henri Gault and Christian Millau's 'Vive la Nouvelle Cuisine Française' (1973) was 'You will eliminate rich sauces.' Michel Guérard in *La Grande cuisine minceur* in 1976 re-engineered sauces with little or no cream, butter or egg yolks to great acclaim, and today many chefs avoid flour liaisons in favour of thickening with arrowroot or potato starch, yogurt, light cream or vegetable purées.

Counterintuitively, sauces made with beurre blanc (emulsified butter and white wine) became spectacularly popular in the 1960s, both for the admirable technique required to make the emulsion hold and the elimination of flour as a thickener, viewed as heavy and pasty. But the new nouvelle cuisine, on the model of Paul Bocuse, depended more on 'integral sauces' made from pan juices or aromatic broths and less on butter, cream and flour for thickening. In the fat-conscious present, sauces are even construed as dangerous to good health. Reminiscent of Magninus in fourteenth-century Milan, Hervé This laments that 'sauces are the gourmand's poison: they make him fat and threaten him . . . with gout and dieting.'[12] A 'sauce moderne', according to Joël Robuchon, is simply a very reduced jus mixed with a bit of butter or cream to emulsify it.[13] The new principle holds that butter thickens without the floury taste of roux-based sauces, but butter has not been banned altogether. As in the transition from medieval to

Duck confit with 'sauce moderne' of lightly thickened jus.

modern sauces, in the 'light' sauce age dietetic principles are accommodated to a point, but taste trumps health.

Composed sauces continued to belong to both domestic and professional kitchens after the systematic changes of the nineteenth century. However, sauce in bourgeois kitchens was necessarily simplified and made more practical. In 1893 Charles Driessens published a series of culinary lectures to housewives in a magazine called *Le Pot-au-feu*, acknowledging that home kitchens could not be expected to have the fonds or glaces available in restaurants. His recipes used a simple roux to replace the building blocks of velouté or espagnole and suggested that the popular Liebig industrial meat extract could replace meat essences. By the early twentieth century, home cookbooks routinely referred to Liebig extract by name as an ingredient in composed sauces. However, women's magazines

Liebig meat extract advertisement, 1890.

of the late nineteenth and early twentieth century in France continued to include complicated sauces in menu suggestions and
assumed that hollandaise sauce, for example, would be familiar
enough to readers that providing a recipe was not necessary.[14]

In his cookbook for American households, *Sauces, French
and Famous* (1951), Louis Diat – inventor of the cold potato
soup vichyssoise and head chef at the Ritz hotels in New York,
Paris and London – gave recipes for only a limited number of
white, brown and cold sauces, but even these recipes required
the cook to first prepare a base sauce and then add juices from
the cooked meat. These standards were a far cry from the
canned mushroom soup used as gravy in American home
cooking of the same era. Twentieth-century American recipes
for French sauces tended to simplify techniques and ingredients or reduce the menu of possibilities. Child followed Diat's
example in *Mastering the Art of French Cooking* (1961), offering
recipes for béchamel, hollandaise and velouté, but not what she
calls the 'brown mother sauce' (espagnole), because it took too
long to prepare. Fannie Farmer simplified béchamel for
American housewives in the early twentieth century as 'white
sauce' with butter, flour and milk, although she kept velouté
and sauce allemande (velouté plus lemon and egg). These
changes point to the informality that distinguished American
home cooking from the French (Child, for example, suggested
that sauce Robert could be served on hamburgers), as well as
the retreat of heavy sauces from the table. Nevertheless, the
1950s heralded the creation of the sauce spoon at the Lasserre
restaurant in Paris, a flat spoon with a notch for piercing aspics
(or preventing the sauce from dripping from the spoon; its
function is debated) meant to enable diners to retrieve sauce
from the plate without tipping it.

One of the most enduring named sauces inhabits both
the elite and the bourgeois realms and transcends culinary eras

in cookbooks and in literary works. Sauce Robert, mainly onions and vinegar, is many centuries old but still has a place in present-day cookbooks. Named after a now-forgotten chef, the sauce was referenced in Taillevent as a boiled mustard sauce for chicken and appeared in La Varenne's *Le Cuisinier françois* seven times as a simple sauce of onion fried in fat from roasted meat, verjuice, vinegar and sometimes mustard. In *Le Quart-livre* (1552) Rabelais called sauce Robert 'healthy and essential' for rabbit, duck, pork, eggs and 'a thousand other meats'.[15] It remains, transformed by the addition of butter and sauce espagnole, in modern cookbooks. As with sauce allemande, sauce Robert became metaphorical in the nine-teenth century, representative of a criticism that Carême and his followers had taken art and invention in cuisine too far. Eneas Sweetland Dallas in *Kettner's Book of the Table* (1877) objected that sauce Robert, once a simple sauce of onions cooked in butter with a bit of mustard and tarragon vinegar, was 'impossible to recognize' in Paris and London, 'its fine gusto lost in a weak civilization'.[16] Materially, Dallas noted that the perversion of the sauce had less onion, added chopped gherkins and was sometimes loaded with wine and ketchup or drenched in vinegar. Spiritually, one can assume that he found these changes emblematic of an unravelling of standards outside the kitchen as well. Dallas maintained that Taillevent stole the sauce from the British, having mistranslated 'Roebuck Sauce' and turned it into sauce Robert.

The metaphorical meaning of sauce Robert resonated with authors of literary texts as well. Faced with a prison meal of black bread, raw onions and old cheese, Danglars in Dumas' *The Count of Monte Cristo* (1846) reminisced not about a specific dish but about the sauce Robert his chef used to prepare. Elegant versions of sauce Robert contain finely chopped onion softened in butter, white wine and demi-glace and are therefore an evolved version of the raw onion that Danglars dismissively calls the 'horrible food of the savage'.[17] The interpretation of this scene depends on the reader's knowledge that sauce Robert is made with onion, and demonstrates that the sauce was familiar enough to be recognized even in shorthand. The civilizing effect of the sauce Robert was also clear in Perrault's seventeenth-century fairy tale *La Belle au bois dormant* (*Sleeping Beauty*). The evil queen with a penchant for eating small children demands to be served the little girl named Aurore for dinner 'à la sauce Robert'. As is her custom, the ogress will consume this meat raw. She requests sauce Robert with her meat, as Louis Marin shows, because she 'wants to apply the art of cooking, the Robert sauce, to its antithesis, raw flesh' in order to legitimize her act of cannibalism.[18] But the hunter sent to dispatch the little girl kills a lamb instead, and the cook serves it to the unsuspecting queen. As a cultural sign, the sauce performs an essential function in making the raw meat edible. For the queen, it makes the culturally inedible (human) meat ingestible because it thus becomes elegant, 'cooked' food and not a barbaric plate of raw child meat. For the hunter, it disguises the raw lamb meat as the little girl the queen wants to consume and saves both his life and the girl's. In either case sauce Robert transforms the meat from something indigestible into a desired food, just as the imagined sauce Robert in Dumas' tale would do for the savage raw onion.

The sauces that resonate in literature are the 'old' sauces, heavy with fat and memory. In his expansive and foodcentric novel *À la recherche du temps perdu*, Marcel Proust used Escoffier's finely wrought sauces to recall the France of bygone days. The third volume of the novel, *Le Côté de Guermantes* (1920), featured staid representations of meals with asparagus sauce mousseline (hollandaise with whipped cream) and leg of lamb à la sauce béarnaise (white wine, tarragon, shallots and emulsified egg yolks) at the Duchesse de Guermantes' table. These dishes are part of a rigidly conservative and elegant cuisine; to the illuminated reader, they reinforce the imagery conveyed by the Guermantes' mansion and their elite dinner parties. There seems to be no idiomatic value in jus or in an unnamed sauce that lacks a connection to the culinary roots of France. In the nouvelle cuisine of the Bocuse era, following the multiplication of new sauce combinations fostered by Escoffier, named dishes reflected the cook's imagination but rarely places or the names of noble families, for obvious cultural reasons. Escoffier transformed fish velouté, for example, with mushroom essence, oyster jus, cream and egg yolks emulsified with butter into sauces with generic names like diplomate, écossaise and régence. This shift in the power of construction takes resonance away from national and institutional identity and connects it to an individual chef. In terms of representation and international identity, these names are less rhetorically valuable. It is hardly surprising that named sauces like espagnole, Robert and béarnaise dominate in literature, since in these cases the sauce's representational value comes from the accumulated centuries of familiarity, the codification of a sauce's meaning. The 'culinary grammar' demanded of a French reader is useless when faced with a reference to a preparation associated with one chef, one restaurant or the single occasion of a meal when a chef creates a sauce *sur place* to correspond exactly to the ingredients at hand, for which the evocative power goes no further than the diner's plate. In the chef-driven era, sauce as metaphor may be replaced by salad, 'the domain of mélange and organized disorder', according to Claude Fischler, who emphasizes the absolute freedom of creativity allowed by salads that encourage innovation and do not hold firm to 'grammatical' rules.[19]

Salad dressing, the sauce for salad, is another vinegar-heavy sauce that has seen a transformation, the modern version departing entirely from dietetic principles that would not have paired 'cold, moist' lettuce and raw vegetables with 'cold, dry' vinegar but rather with 'hot' salt or oil. Vinegar was therefore used sparingly in early salad dressings, but it was present. There is some evidence that vinaigrettes prepared with mustard existed in late antiquity, and recipes in *Apicius* used *garum* and oil to sauce raw herbs. Pierre de Ronsard spoke of a dressing of salt, vinegar and French olive oil for fresh herbs in 'La Salade' (1568), a poem endorsing the medicinal value of natural food. A sixteenth-century French proverb approved of salt and oil but discouraged vinegar: 'Salad washed and salted well, not much vinegar and lots of oil.'[20] First used as a sauce for meat in *Le Ménagier de Paris* (*c.* 1393), the French term 'vinaigrette' is faithful to its main ingredient, and traditional French salad dressing remains an emulsion of oil, vinegar, mustard and salt prepared just before the salad is dressed. Louis xiv was particularly fond of salads dressed with salt and vinegar, although lettuce and certain raw vegetables were considered particularly hard to digest and his doctors eventually forbade him to eat them. Massialot and Menon included recipes for basic salad dressings with oil and vinegar in their eighteenth-century cookbooks, although the greens were sometimes cooked.

By the nineteenth century, as with most sauces, the palette of ingredients for salad dressing had expanded enormously. In the *Physiologie du goût* (Physiology of Taste, 1825), Jean-Anthelme Brillat-Savarin sang the praises of a 'fashionable salad maker' named D'Albignac who had made his fortune in London and elsewhere by bringing the French art of salad to the world.[21] He carried with him a 'carrik' of salad dressing ingredients: flavoured vinegars, oils, soy, caviar, truffles, anchovies, 'calchup', meat jus and egg yolks, the essential ingredient in mayonnaise. In *The Cook's Oracle*, William Kitchiner described a similar 'Sauce Box' of 'flavouring materials' meant to be portable so that sauces could be improvised on the spot. Kitchiner's box contained walnut pickle, mushroom 'catsup', powders, mustard, soy sauce and 'salad sauce', which appeared to be a sauce gribiche with hard-boiled egg yolks, mustard, vinegar and oil, although he noted that cream could replace the oil. Elizabeth David illuminated the history of ignominious 'English Salad Sauce' (or salad cream) by observing that the original recipe was 'honourable', meant to be served on cooked vegetable salads or fish salads, not lettuce or green salads. The original 'salad sauce' with cooked egg yolks and cream became commercial salad cream applied to lettuce, and 'remains one of the major culinary disasters of this country . . . which make English

Vinaigrette sauce for salad. Vinaigrettes depend on two ancient ingredients: vinegar and mustard.

salad sauces, creams, and so-called mayonnaise the laughing stock of Europe'.[22]

Early American salad dressings used salt, sugar, vinegar, melted butter, molasses and occasionally olive oil (an expensive commodity in colonial America). Salad was generally considered food for the upper class in nineteenth-century America, and garlic was found only in dressings in French restaurants, with the notable exception of Caesar Cardini's restaurants in Tijuana, in 1924 the birthplace of the Caesar salad. Cardini insisted that only Italian olive oil and imported parmesan cheese be used and, contrary to popular belief, did not include anchovies in the dressing. Nearly 90 years later, Marzetti trademarked the Cardini name and now sells a line of Cardini's salad dressings, including the unfortunately named 'Roasted Asian Sesame Dressing'. The 'Original Caesar Dressing' description claims that 'there is nothing like an original and Cardini's Caesar Salad Dressing is the original', but the dressing contains soybean oil, olive oil, parmesan cheese, egg yolk and anchovies, among other things. Bottled salad dressings began to appear in America in the 1870s, and the favourite American salad dressing flavour is currently ranch, a creamy sauce with garlic and herbs created by Hidden Valley Ranch in the 1970s. This is a deeply American sauce with no real equivalent elsewhere. The first bottled salad dressing sold by Kraft was in fact 'French Dressing', a tomato-red, sweet and tangy sauce with no relation at all to the French or their salad sauces.

4
Gravy: Sauce for Meat, Sauce for Pasta

The term 'gravy' is as least as complicated as the word 'sauce', since its meaning has changed over time and it encompasses a number of preparations, from simple meat juices to a dressing built from meat essences and foundational sauces. The defining ingredient that makes a sauce a gravy is meat. As a cooked sauce for (and usually made from) meat, gravy is firmly entrenched in British and American cookery. Mexican *moles* function as a kind of gravy by this definition, and Italian sauces for pasta belong to this category by way of the tomato. Early tomato sauces for meat led to Italian tomato sauce for pasta and the Italian-American tomato-meat sauce called, not coincidentally, gravy.

Gravy by its nature belongs to home cooking. Although by strict definition meat gravies may be present on elite tables, gravy generally aligns with middle-class or low food. This sauce principally belongs to the British, first by virtue of the word itself and second because of the British admiration for pragmatic cookery. The term 'gravy' is derived from a fourteenth-century term for meat or fish bouillon (or meat served in its own sauce) spelled interchangeably *grané* and *gravé* in French manuscripts of the period, including *Le Ménagier de Paris* and *Le Viandier*.[1] Reinforcing the connection to meat, *grané* appears to come from the Old French term *grain*, meaning, in the culinary sense, either the liquid from grain or fruit (like verjuice) used to sauce meat or the solid part (the meat) of a dish with solid and liquid components. Therefore 'gravy' is a sauce made from meat to be served with meat. Beginning in the seventeenth century, French sauces evolved into secondary preparations from the main dish, often distinctly separate from the cooked meat. But British sauces, and American sauces in the British model, kept the meat – usually a joint or roast – central, and gravy therefore is more at home across the English Channel from its apparent origin than in France. British gravies also represent a purposeful rejection of French culinary practices, precisely the ones that distinguish French sauces from British gravies: the use of precious ingredients, the fuss of multiple steps and the quantity of meats used in essences and coulis to sauce a single dish. For this reason, gravies tend to belong to humble, non-aristocratic cooking. 'High' sauces, even in British cooking, tend to follow the French model.

Gravy (spelled 'gravey') appeared in *The Forme of Cury* (*c.* 1390), the earliest known British cookbook, compiled by cooks to Richard II, but these recipes were quite different from the thickened sauces that now carry the name. Recipes for 'chykens in gravey' and 'oysters in gravey' were characteristically meat-heavy, based on boiled meat and broth, thickened with almonds and full of spices. Non-gravy sauces (spelled 'sawse' or 'sawce') contained many of the same ingredients (almonds, bread, herbs and spices, and sometimes the fat from the cooked meat), plus vinegar or wine, but these sauces were prepared separately from the meat and poured over it or served alongside it. Seventeenth-century concoctions of meat drippings, fruit and spices adhered to the spirit of 'gravy' if not always the name. Gervase Markham's recipe for 'Sauce for a Stubble Goose' in *The English Huswife* (1615) included roasted apples, vinegar, goose dripping, barberries, breadcrumbs, sugar and cinnamon. Robert May's *The Accomplisht Cook* (1660) offered a 'Sauce for Land-fowl' containing puréed, boiled prunes, chicken dripping, cinnamon, ginger, sugar and salt. May used the term 'gravy' to mean juices from cooked meat or fish, sometimes extracted with a wooden press, made into a sauce for the same meat or saved for use as an ingredient in cold meat dishes. Sauces made with this gravy were thickened with bread, ground almonds, egg yolks or beaten butter and infused with strong flavours, frequently including ginger, mace, cinnamon, cloves and pepper. Hannah Glasse and William Kitchiner used the term 'gravy' for meat juices as well as the thickened sauce made from them.

Early British gravies retained some medieval characteristics, using strong spices borrowed from the Middle East and pairing meat with fruit, while French *sauciers* distanced themselves from heavy spices and the contrast of sweet and savoury in favour of

Worcester Porcelain Factory sauceboat showing the Four Ages of Man, *c.* 1756.

more delicate herbs and an alignment of flavours between sauce and meat. Colin Spencer offers a theological reason: after the English Reformation in the 1530s, composed dishes with sauces and fancy preparations for fast days were deemed French and associated with Catholicism.[2] Loyal British cooks steeped in anti-French and anti-Catholic sentiment shunned French recipes and began to insist on more 'natural' cooking methods: large cuts of roasted meat accompanied by simple gravy from the meat juices. 'Made dishes' of meat or fish covered with a complicated sauce were considered French and therefore suspicious, although chefs like Robert May who apprenticed in France returned these sauces to British tables a century later. But the aversion to French sauces, and the preference for meat served whole with a sauce passed around the table in a sauceboat, shaped British cuisine in a fundamental way from this moment forward. In addition, Spencer argues that the Puritan age and the growth of the bourgeoisie in the seventeenth century enabled the success of female cookbook writers who favoured practical cooking that included gravy.

With nine recipes for gravy in four chapters, Hannah Glasse made an all-out effort to show the efficacy of British cooking and the frivolity of fancy French sauces in *The Art of Cookery*. Glasse included five recipes for 'cullis' (the English word for coulis) and called for ham essence and cullis in a recipe for partridge ragoût that she then called 'an odd jumble of trash' and did not recommend making, her way of insinuating that French sauces were unnecessarily costly. She likened the sauce to 'boiling a leg of mutton in champaign' as the ingredients were so wasteful and illogical. In a gravy recipe that she did endorse, Glasse used the term 'gravy meat', new to the eighteenth century, for cuts of meat that lent themselves particularly well to gravy-making, although she offered alternatives for those on a less generous budget. Proper gravy for Glasse was fairly generic and served many purposes; her 'To Make Gravy' recipe ended with the assurance that 'this will do for most things'.

In the mindset of the eighteenth-century British bourgeois cook, fancy sauces were impractical and expensive, imprudent, even heretical, if the religious argument were taken far enough. Other female cookbook writers followed in Glasse's footsteps, disdaining or ignoring French techniques in favour of simple, 'honest' gravies. British cookbooks of the seventeenth century did not use flour or roux to thicken sauces and even the eighteenth-century recipes favoured *beurre manié* (butter mixed with flour) or flour stirred into liquid. Instead of coulis, many eighteenth-century English cooks added spicy, pungent ketchups and pickles to gravies for meat and fish to create a distinctly English cuisine that was purposely distanced from the French. Susannah Carter's *The Frugal Housewife*, published in London in 1765, lies somewhere in the middle. Frugal or not, Carter gave a recipe for veal gravy with essence of ham, and a beef gravy deglazed with strong broth, claret and white wine, finished with anchovy and herbs. Rather than develop flavour with essences or coulis, cooks like Elizabeth

Limehouse Porcelain Manufactory sauceboat, *c.* 1745.

Raffald (*The Experienced English Housekeeper*, 1769) and Isabella Beeton (*The Book of Household Management*, 1859) suggested the use of 'browning' to add colour to sauces. Raffald's recipe began with melted butter and sugar cooked until brown, with red wine and the usual flavourings of cloves, mace, pepper, mushroom ketchup and lemon rind. Beeton's contained burned sugar and water but none of the flavourings of the previous century's version. Browning sauces still exist under the trade names Kitchen Bouquet and Gravy Master, both American products, and they still serve the same purpose: to

For EXTRA-RICH
BROWN DELICIOUS
GRAVY

Use
KITCHEN
Bouquet

It's easy to make your gravy *extra*-rich, *extra*-brown, *extra*-delicious every time. Just stir in Kitchen Bouquet! Ah! What rich, brown color and how it brings out that true meat taste! Adds no artificial flavor. Good cooks have used Kitchen Bouquet for over 70 years.
COSTS SO LITTLE.

Kitchen Bouquet
advertisement,
1950.

add colour but not necessarily flavour to meat and gravies. Kitchen Bouquet emerged in the 1880s and Gravy Master dates from 1935; both are essentially composed of sugar, aromatics and spices.

Cookbooks following Glasse's model were meant for a bourgeois audience and seem to confirm Spencer's claim that female cooks leaned toward the pragmatic. High-status chefs like Vincent La Chapelle and Louis-Eustache Ude, both French emigrants working in Britain, defended the French (aristocratic) approach to sauces. In *The Modern Cook* (1733), La Chapelle instructed cooks to thicken sauces with flour and not breadcrumbs, and to use sauce espagnole as a base for other sauces. In the nineteenth century the British elite idolized French cuisine and disdained British food, while the less prosperous middle classes came to embrace British cooking, and roast meat with gravy made from meat dripping was consumed almost daily at the main meal. William Kitchiner put financially prudent British gravies in a more refined context in *The Cook's Oracle*. He exclaimed that his recipe for 'Beef Gravy Sauce with Mushrooms' 'far exceeds the most costly gravies of the French' and that another gravy 'at a very moderate Expense, and without much trouble' was 'equal to the most costly Consommé of the Parisian Kitchen'.[3] This gravy was refined enough to be served at a formal dinner, a pint of it in a sauceboat at either end of the table, as the recipe instructed. To finish the sauce, the cook was told to 'preserve *the intrinsic Gravy* which flows from the meat, in the Argyll'.[4] An 'argyll' or 'argyle' is a nineteenth-century British term for a gravy boat with an inner reservoir for hot water to keep the gravy warm at table. British recipes of the period commonly insisted that gravy or sauce be served in a sauce-boat or basin (and thus separate from the meat), perhaps an extension of the antipathy toward French 'made dishes' that

Victorian silver argyle (gravy pot), London, 1856. The outer chamber holds gravy and the inner chamber hot water to keep the gravy warm.

arrived at table fancifully sauced. Susannah Carter's recipe for roast venison, for example, advised the cook to 'put no gravy in the dish but send it in one boat and currant jelly, melted, in another'; for turkey, there should be 'good gravy in a boat, and bread, onion or oyster sauce in a basin'.[5] At formal and modest dinners alike, table settings included designated containers for gravy and sauces.

The middle-class British (and later American) cook's desire to avoid waste, born out of the Victorian era, popularized recipes for cold meat dishes that required gravy. Hash or hodge-podge, a mixture of leftover meats with leftover vegetables and gravy, turned up regularly on British tables as a way to use up the Sunday roast; Alexis Soyer (another expat French chef under Ude) called his recipe 'Remains'. Spencer laments this turn for the worse in British cooking by noting that scraps that would have been fed to pigs in France or, in another era, in Britain, 'were thrust beneath a floury sauce, reheated, and sent up to the nursery'.[6] In a twentieth-century study, the anthropologist Mary Douglas showed that gravy is an essential part of the pattern of British meals. Each standard main meal replicates the elements of Sunday dinner: a 'centre-piece' of meat, 'trimmings' of one or two green vegetables, a serving of potato and 'a sousing in rich, brown, thickened gravy'.[7] Special meals might increase the number of trimmings or dressings, but a main meal 'cannot be recognised as a meal in the system unless its first course is constituted on these rules. Some elements can be duplicated, but none omitted.'[8] That is, in Douglas's terms, without gravy, there is no meal. The 'gravy rule' applies even to the sweet course, where the centre becomes fruit or cake and the 'gravy' is custard or cream 'poured over the plate in the way gravy is used in the first course'.[9]

Many middle-class American cookbooks of the eighteenth and early nineteenth centuries were simply copies of previous British cookbooks or revised editions with an attempt to include local flora and fauna. For this reason, gravy played much the same role in American home cooking of the period as it did in Britain. Amelia Simmons's *American Cookery* (1798), the first cookbook printed in America by an American cook, included gravy recipes thickened with butter and flavoured with ketchups as well as a number of fruit sauces and pickles. A century later, Fannie Farmer's *The Boston Cooking-school Cookbook* (1896) raised the bar somewhat with a number of named French sauces simplified for home cooks, including espagnole, velouté and a Champagne sauce for ham that would have infuriated Hannah Glasse: the main ingredients were reduced espagnole, Champagne and powdered sugar.

Nevertheless, true to her Puritan roots, Farmer retained a section on cold (leftover) meat dishes served with gravy and an all-purpose gravy recipe in the poultry chapter. The 1953 edition of Irma Rombauer's *Joy of Cooking* (originally published by Bobbs-Merrill in 1931) classified sauces and gravies together but gravies were treated first. Rombauer offered techniques for three kinds of gravy – one made with pan drippings, another for stews and a third for roasts – and like Beeton and Raffald before her suggested that gravy be coloured with caramel or a commercial browning product. The 1950s heralded the advent of gravies made from canned condensed soup and ready-made canned gravies for housewives without the time or inclination to make proper gravy for the family meal. Gravy for roasted meat is now generally relegated to the holiday table in the u.s., often reheated from a jar or can.

The tomato can be seen as the transitional ingredient that led from meat gravy to gravy (or sauce) for Italian pasta. The

Bisto gravy granules advertisement, 1945. A meat-flavoured gravy starter introduced in the UK in 1908, the product was named Bisto because it 'Browns, Seasons, and Thickens in One'.

tomato belonged to the language of European cuisines 'only after its morphological reduction into something familiar, in this case a sauce, which made it fully compatible with traditional usages, while at the same time introducing a new note of taste and color'.[10] Tomatoes were used in sauce for meat centuries before tomato sauce was paired with pasta, however. The first reference to cooked tomatoes is in an Italian source, Petrus Andreas Matthiolus's botanical guide of 1554. The earliest recipe for tomato sauce in European sources, a spicy sauce for boiled meats, appeared in Naples in 1692 in Antonio Latini's *Lo scalco alla moderna*. Vincenzo Corrado's *Il cuoco galante* (1773) included tomato sauces for veal, sturgeon, lobster and eggs. Similarly, the first references to tomato sauce in British and American sources in the early nineteenth century were sauces for meat (or 'gravy'), including Richard Alsop's recipe for 'Tomato or Love-Apple Sauce' (*The Universal Receipt Book*, 1814) and N.K.M. Lee's four recipes for tomato sauce in *The Cook's Own Book* (1832). Recipes for 'Tomatas with Gravy' and 'Tomata Sauce for Cold Meat' appeared in 1826 in *The Gardener's Magazine* in London. In 1842, an article in *The American Agriculturist* in New York noted that tomatoes could be cooked for 'sauce, for catsup or gravy, for meat and for pies'.[11] Early American sauces with tomato tended to be vinegar-based meat sauces, similar to the British ketchups discussed in chapter Two. The transition from New World to Old World for the tomato in Mediterranean cuisine hinged on the use of chillies.

It may seem blasphemous to label *mole poblano* a gravy, but it is at base a sauce for meat and it bridges the Old and New Worlds just as tomato gravy does. *Mole* also aligns linguistically with 'gravy' as a generic term that takes on specific meanings depending on ingredients and context. The term *mole* comes from the Nahuatl word *molli*, meaning sauce; by extension, guacamole is sauce from avocados, and the *molcajete* common in Mexican kitchens is a bowl for preparing sauce by grinding or mashing ingredients. *Mole* refers to a group of Mexican sauces that combine indigenous and colonial ingredients. The best known of these, *mole poblano*, is a spicy, complex sauce cooked with turkey, another food native to Mexico. Sometimes called the Mexican national dish, legend has it that *mole* was created in the late seventeenth century by Mexican nuns of the Puebla de los Angeles, who blended Old World spices and New World chillies and tomatoes with chocolate, nuts and seeds to make a new kind of sauce. The truth is murkier, since there were a limited number of Latin American cookbooks published before the nineteenth century. The inclusion of chocolate in the cooked sauce excludes it from Aztec heritage; chocolate was consumed by the Aztecs exclusively as a ceremonial drink. Historians have variously attributed the origins of *mole* to Spanish missionaries, pre-Columbian indigenous cuisine and the cooks of seventeenth-century New Spain (Mexico), and it seems evident that the sauce resulted from some combination of these influences. The Old World spices (cinnamon, cloves, black pepper) combined with meat mimicked medieval recipes favoured by the aristocratic Spanish colonizers; native cooks taught newcomers to add chilli peppers and pumpkin seeds to European sauces and stews; and the pork fat, garlic and coriander essential to the recipe came directly from Spain. Nineteenth-century cookbooks gave recipes for *moles* from Puebla and Oaxaca, but generally only for one Oaxacan *mole*, the black *mole* that closely resembled the original Pueblan sauce.[12] There are a number of regional *moles* including yellow and green varieties, all cooked sauces served with meat. *Mole poblano* is now generally served at celebrations and holiday meals, but regional *moles* have a place in everyday cuisine.

Molcajete with guacamole. The *molcajete* is a traditional kitchen implement in Mexican cooking, similar in form and use to the mortarium used to prepare sauce bases in ancient Greece and Rome.

The Spanish returning from colonies in Mexico brought a taste for tomatoes and chillies to Europe. In sixteenth-century Aztec sauces, the tomato was subordinate to red and green chillies. Latini's recipe for 'Tomato Sauce, Spanish-style' was published in Naples when Naples was still part of the Spanish Empire; the sauce contained chillies as a seasoning, but tomato was primary. In Juan de la Mata's *Arte de repostería* (1747), 'Spanish-style' sauce seems to have shed its Aztec roots in a recipe identical to Latini's but without chillies.[13] Italian cooks resisted the change a bit longer, since Corrado's Neapolitan sauces '*alla spagnuola*' (Spanish-style) and '*di pomidoro*' (with tomato) both call for red pepper. These recipes are all sauces for meats, hinting at the transition from gravy for meat to sauce for pasta in the following century. Corrado's other sauces for meat carry recognizable names, if not the expected ingredients. An early form of pesto served with veal kidneys contained pistachios, spices and lemon juice but no herbs; a sauce 'alla cacciatore' with wine, garlic and spices and bound with breadcrumbs bears no resemblance to the current *cacciatore* with tomatoes, red wine and onions; but the ubiquitous sauce Robert (called 'salsa Roberta') is fairly true to form, with onions, butter, capers, coriander and wine. Corrado's eighteenth-century cookbook shows that the Italians were somewhat behind the French in terms of sauce innovation, with its fifteen 'colì' (coulis) recipes, most thickened with toasted bread.

The debut of tomato sauce on pasta in Italy is the subject of much debate; the dish was likely known in Italy as early as the 1820s.[14] Printed recipes for pasta with tomatoes first appeared in Ippolito Cavalcanti's *Cucina teorico-pratica* (The Theory and Practice of Cooking, 1837) and *Cucina casareccia in dialetto napoletano* (Home Cooking in the Neapolitan Dialect, 1839). The earlier book contained a number of sauces for meat as well, with and without tomato, including 'salsa all'Italiana' with mushrooms, white wine, 'sugo colato' (strained 'master' sauce) and 'salsa alla Spagnuolo' with turnip, parsnip and coriander plus white wine and the master sauce. The expected tomato sauce for meat contains parsley, basil and tomatoes cooked in butter. Tomato sauces for pasta are more prevalent in Cavalcanti's *Cucina casareccia*, marking a distinction between the food for the upper classes (principally characterized by meat) in the former book and for the modest classes in the latter, in which tomato sauce dresses vermicelli and macaroni as well as frittatas, beans and *baccalà*. Because of the number of references to tomatoes in these recipes for home cooking, it seems likely that Southern Italians of the lower classes were eating pasta with tomato sauce earlier but that such sauces did not appear in published cookbooks until Cavalcanti. By the time Pellegrino Artusi published *La scienza in cucina* in 1891, the first attempt at a national cookbook for Italy, tomato sauce had become so ubiquitous in Italy that he prefaced his 'salsa di pomodoro' recipe with an anecdote about a nosy priest whose constant intrusions on private affairs earned him the nickname 'Don Pomodoro' (Sir Tomato) to show that 'tomatoes go in everything'.[15] True to its reputation, Artusi's tomato sauce could be served with meat and with pasta.

Artusi's cookbook attempted to fix Italian cooking as an entity but still included some regional identifications: maca- roni with sardines *alla siciliana*, two recipes for macaroni *alla napoletana* with tomatoes and macaroni *alla bolognese* with veal and cream but no tomatoes. There were hints of a rivalry with French sauces, such as the note that Italian *balsamella* was just as good as French béchamel but less complicated, although it is the same sauce. Another major national cookbook arrived in 1929, Ada Boni's *Il talismano della felicità*, but it included only two tomato sauces for pasta and credited *besciamella* to Louis de Béchamel. Despite the bold claim in her introduction that there is no such thing as 'Italian cooking', Marcella Hazan struck a patriotic tone in her *Classic Italian Cook Book* (1973), noting that 'béchamel, despite its name, is a thoroughly Italian sauce', known in Romagna as *balsamella* 'long before the French christened it béchamel'.[16] By all available evidence, it seems that béchamel belongs to the French, even if it can also function as a 'thoroughly Italian sauce' in context. Sauces are closely tied to national pride and culinary identity, an idea that will be considered in the final chapter.

Specific names for sauces in Italian cuisine, like names for pasta, depend on the region in which they originated and the ingredients they contain. Genoa's pesto with basil first appeared in print in the cookbook *Vera cuciniera genovese* (1863), although recipes with similar ingredients were in circulation centuries earlier, including Martino's fifteenth-century recipe for a sauce with parmesan, fresh cheese and rocket (arugula).[17] Pesto made with basil as a sauce for pasta remained relatively unknown outside Liguria until the late twentieth century. The date of origin for other sauces for pasta is difficult to determine because their regional character kept them from being widely known until regional cookbooks began to appear in the nineteenth century, around the time of national unification in 1861. In addition, as a mainly low-status food until at least the eighteenth century, pasta did not normally appear in cookbooks meant for wealthier households. Some of the well-known sauces were certainly consumed in lower-class households for centuries before recipes were standardized in modern (nineteenth-century or later) cookbooks, but because they were not part of high cuisine there is no primer on Italian pasta sauces akin to Escoffier or the *Répertoire de la cuisine*.

Unlike French sauces, it is difficult to trace the evolution of Italian pasta sauces from their early forms to their current incarnations and much of their history depends on myth.

Carlo Brogi (1850–1925), *Maccheroni Seller in Naples*, photograph.

Spaghetti *alla carbonara* with *guanciale*, garlic, beaten eggs and parmesan or pecorino was supposedly a hearty meal for the coal miners of Lazio and Abruzzo, the regions to which it is linked. The Italian actor Ugo Tognazzi chose spaghetti *alla carbonara* for a dinner in New York at the premiere of his film *Marcia nuziale* in 1966, attended by a mostly American audience. He rejected tomato sauce as too base and ragù as too familiar but thought a sauce of eggs and bacon would best fit American tastes; however, in an act of 'Italian culinary chauvinism', Tognazzi felt it necessary to 'Americanize' the simple sauce with the addition of cream and wine to bring it closer to his guests' food traditions, heavy with fat and alcohol.[18] The Abruzzan town of Amatrice is nominatively the home of sauce *all'amatriciana* (with *guanciale*, tomatoes, chillies and pecorino) served on bucatini or perciatelli (hollow spaghetti). Spaghetti *aglio e olio* belongs to Rome and despite its humble ingredients (olive oil and garlic) it is now a favourite of chic young Romans who stop at a trattoria for a *spaghettata* (spaghetti snack) during a long night out, presumably followed by strong breath mints. *Cacio e pepe* sauce, simply grated cheese with black pepper and a bit of water from the pasta pot, reflects the poverty and simplicity of the food in seventeenth-century Naples where the sauce originated, when plain or lightly dressed pasta sometimes served as the only meal of the day. On the other end of the spectrum, Alfredo sauce for fettuccine is rich with cream, butter and cheese and was ceremoniously tossed with a gold fork and spoon at the eponymous Roman restaurant where it was created in 1914. It has been gluttonously reappropriated by numerous Italian-American restaurants, some of which offer unlimited servings of this already over-the-top sauce. Ragù is the celebrated meaty sauce of Bologna and a slow-cooked meat dish served with short pasta in Naples, similar in name and character to the French *ragoût*. If it is true to its heritage, ragù from Bologna should not contain tomatoes, according to Gillian Riley, since 'Bologna, *la dotta e la grassa*, had a name for intellectual rigor and good living long before the tomato came along to muddy the waters and add what is not necessarily a helpful dimension to a rich meat sauce.'[19] But many recipes for ragù include the New World fruit, including Hazan's, which calls for milk, white wine and canned tomatoes. Furthermore, Hazan defended tomato sauce in a 1995 revision of her earlier cookbooks, claiming that 'no flavor expresses more clearly the genius of Italian cooks than the freshness, the immediacy, the richness of good tomatoes adroitly matched with the most suitable choice of pasta.'[20]

Vocabulary adds another layer of difficulty in the history of pasta sauce, as there are numerous words for sauce in Italian, including *sugo* and *salsa*. Eighteenth-century Italian cookbooks, including Corrado's and Francesco Leonardi's *L'Apicio moderno* (1790), followed the French model to a point with recipes for *culì* or *colì* as a base for other sauces. Leonardi offered a *culì di pomidoro* that imitated other contemporary Italian tomato-based sauces for meat but gave *culì* as an ingredient (one of the meat bases, although he did not specify which one). Cavalcanti used *sugo* to indicate a master sauce, something like sauce espagnole, and *salsa* for meat and pasta sauces. Artusi distinguished between *sugo*, a master sauce or coulis, and *salsa*, a prepared sauce with aromatics and fresh herbs. Among the four *sugo* recipes by Artusi, *sugo di pomodoro* consisted simply of cooked, strained tomatoes and *sugo di carne* was said to be called *salsa spagnuolo* by the French, clearly an adoption of sauce espagnole. Artusi referred to pasta sauce as an *intingolo*, as distinct from the *salse* that were most often intended for meat. The noun *intingolo* is derived from the verb *intingere*, 'to dip in a liquid', a curious usage in the context of

Spaghetti *alla carbonara*, a hearty sauce for pasta made from bacon (or *guanciale*), eggs and cheese.

pasta, as dictionary definitions suggest that the word is more appropriate for the liquid in which meat is cooked or which emanates from roasted meat (a jus). *Intingolo* can also mean, generically, any sauce. As in cooking, however, the codified 'recipe' does not always reflect common practice: many Italians use *salsa* as the generic term for sauce (meat or condiment) and *sugo* for pasta, and *intingolo* appears to be rare, although regional variations abound. Boni used *salsa* for the master sauces (except for *sugo d'umido*, concentrated beef or pork gravy) and condiment sauces (vinegar or egg-based), but called pasta sauce a *condimento*, following the Italian idea that sauce should dress pasta but not drown it. Boni's *sugo d'umido* is encoded; the literal translation is 'damp sauce' or 'stew sauce' and no recipe is given, as if the cook were expected to have *sugo d'umido* at the ready. For her part, Hazan notes that *sugo* is the right word for pasta sauce but that it is untranslatable. Even on the linguistic level, 'sauce' is complex and subject to misunderstandings and mistranslations.

A vermicelli dish with tomatoes from Cavalcanti's Neapolitan cookbook *Cucina teorico-pratica* is believed to be the first published recipe in which tomatoes are served with pasta. The 'timpano di vermicelli' consisted of layers of halved raw tomatoes and raw vermicelli topped with lard or butter and baked. This same recipe appeared, unchanged and uncredited, in *Simple Italian Cookery* (1912), one of the first Italian cookbooks to appear in the U.S., penned under the Italianate pseudonym Antonia Isola by Mabel Earl McGinnis, an American living in Rome. The tomato figured heavily in McGinnis's recipes, although she suggested that cooks who were unable to find tomato purée substitute it with fresh or canned tomatoes, indicating that this essential element of tomato purée was not yet in widespread use. Her sauce recipes often used Italian names, and she called attention to the regional character of some recipes, such as 'Sicilian Macaroni with Eggplant' and the timbale of vermicelli, a 'Neapolitan Receipt'. Early in its use in America, tomato sauce for pasta was sometimes attributed to Naples, as in Sarah Rutledge's recipe for 'Macaroni a la Napolitana' in *The Carolina Housewife* (1847), but the association was hardly universal at first. In Lee's British-American *The Cook's Own Book* of 1832, 'Macaroni Napolitaine' was baked macaroni and cheese with gravy instead of milk. By the 1930s Italian publications were routinely using the Neapolitan designation for tomato sauces, including Boni's 'vermicelli alla napoletana'.

In present-day America tomato sauce is called 'marinara sauce', 'spaghetti sauce' or even '(red) gravy' in certain regions, and it is by far the most popular sauce for pasta in restaurants and at home. The term 'spaghetti sauce' for tomato sauce, in wide use from the 1950s to the 1980s, demonstrates that Americans wholeheartedly adopted a single sauce for a single pasta, a contrast to the Italian tradition of regional sauces, each paired with the appropriate type of pasta. No dish is more Italian-American than Sunday 'gravy' or meat sauce, as its creation dates from the arrival of Italian immigrants to New York and other u.s. cities where their relative wealth as labourers and the availability of abundant food shaped their eating habits. Italian immigrants to the u.s. consumed meat more often than they had in Italy and purchased more of the foods they had eaten at home: olive oil, vegetables, cheeses and cured meats. Sicilian-American gravy is heavy with meat and 'gravy' is therefore understandable as a term that connects early tomato sauces for meat to pasta sauce. More than a sauce, Italian-American gravy is a demonstration of economic success via food, as it may contain sausages, pork chops or ribs, meatballs and stuffed beef rolls (*braciole*, another new Italian-American food). Recipes for 'Sunday gravy' are as varied as the cooks who make it, but they offer a revealing shorthand for the meaning of the dish. Some list specific cuts of meat and others dispense with specifics and cut to the chase, listing 'two pounds of meat' or 'fried meat' in the ingredients. The emphasis is on richness and quantity, exemplified by meat and plenty of it, a food that was often out of reach in the old country but accessible in the new.

In its New World form, tomato gravy remained tied to the insular Italian family and community structure, especially as the centrepiece of Sunday dinner, a ritual that emphasized the family and created the illusion of a long-standing tradition in a new country. Sunday dinner allowed Italians in America to display hospitality with food and to make a show of food, a practice unavailable to their counterparts in working-class Southern Italy. Recipes for 'Sunday gravy' are often family secrets, committed to Nonna's memory and rarely shared. When they appear in print, they are generally found in locally published cookbooks linked to a parish or community event. Because of the scarcity of published recipes, it is difficult to pinpoint the exact moment that tomato gravy appeared, but despite stories that these recipes are centuries old and were brought from the old country, it is clear that Sunday gravy is a product of late nineteenth-century America and the confluence of factors that allowed Italian immigrants to combine their food traditions with new opportunities for family celebrations and access to higher-status food. The connection to the Old World in recipes for gravy is not a literal but a symbolic one. Corrado's *Il cuoco galante* pinpointed the entry of pasta into high cuisine with his recipe for *timballo di maccheroni*, macaroni sauced with beef gravy, sausage ragù, pork and prosciutto, served in a pastry crust. Savoury pies served as demonstrations of wealth on aristocratic tables beginning in the early Middle Ages. For working-class Italians newly arrived in America, the ingredients remained the same but the covering disappeared; the symbol was transformed into an open display of meat and pasta on a platter, a more appropriate presentation for the demonstrative American culture that allowed upward mobility in a way that was impossible in Italy.

Truly industrial sauce in the u.s. retains a connection to Italian-American sauce of the late nineteenth century and is in fact a product of the unification of regional Italian food by immigrants into one marketable version of 'Italian cuisine'. What was once part of a weekly dinner is now relegated to special occasions as more American cooks choose commercial tomato sauce for family dinners. The most popular commercial pasta sauce in the u.s. is currently Ragú (sic) 'Old World Style' sauce, created in 1937 in Rochester, New York, by Giovanni and Assunta Cantisano, immigrants from Bisticci, Italy. But Ragú is not Italian. It was marked as American by its reversed accent and its designation as 'spaghetti sauce' – the universal sauce for pasta on American tables – on labels from 1969 to 1992. Like other Italian-American immigrant food customs, it participates in an invented Italian pedigree, likely named after Bolognese ragù because Bologna is renowned for its sauce, but this sauce has no relation to the regional character of that specific dish. American-style Ragú is all tomato and no meat, at least in the 'Traditional' and 'Marinara' flavours. The only connection to Italian ragù is the image on the label – a Venetian gondola, still present even after the 'That's Italian!' slogan disappeared in 1992. Tomato sauce likely arrived in America from Southern Italy, not Bologna or Venice, but the cartoon gondola successfully transmits 'Italian' to an American public thanks to early immigrants who created a unified vision of Italian cuisine out of necessity in late nineteenth-century America.[21] The symbolic

Ragú label, 1968, when the sauce was still called 'spaghetti sauce' and not 'pasta sauce' as it is now labelled.

Commercial 'Sicilian gravy' in a jar minus the meat, a curious adaptation since meat is the focus of the traditional Italian-American Sunday tomato sauce.

character of Italian-American pasta sauce is so effective that even a sauce without the symphony of meats deemed necessary to 'gravy' (indeed without any meat at all) can still carry the label. An American supermarket chain now sells meat-free 'Sicilian Gravy' in a jar in its line of house-brand pasta sauces.

Sunday gravy or marinara is the most widespread Italian-American version of tomato sauce for pasta, but there are other American variations, including 'red gravy' in New Orleans (also known as 'Creole gravy'), which has Creole touches: a roux, peppers and hot sauce. Like the muffuletta sandwich of cured meats and olive relish, it is an outgrowth of the merging of Italian immigrant cultures with New Orleans foodways in the nineteenth century. Tomato sauce existed in Creole cuisine before the Sicilian immigrants arrived, but with the Italian influence it came to be served over pasta rather than on meat with rice. There are also recipes for tomato gravy in Southern American cuisine that are literal gravies served on biscuits, rice or potatoes but not pasta, often as a breakfast dish. These sauces generally begin with a roux of bacon fat and flour and use diced tomatoes with tomato juice, water or milk for liquid. Many of the recipe descriptions insist on the Southernness and the heritage of these preparations, served at 'mama's table' just as the Italian-American equivalent insists on the connection to Nonna.

5
Odd Sauces

Most sauces occupy a fixed category, belong to a family of similar sauces and have a clearly defined use. Because sauce is in essence superfluous to eating, it is necessarily a product of innovation and creativity. While formal classifications exist for sauces, quite a number of them defy classification and stretch the limits of sauce-ness. Dessert sauces can be counted as odd, being relatively few in number and common only since the eighteenth century, when the dessert course was more or less in place. Classic French named sauces are mostly intelligible as representative of a historical figure or a particular ingredient, but some sauces bear complicated or disputed etymologies, as with Welsh rarebit, or hold fast to their legendary origins in spite of evidence to the contrary, as with crème Chantilly. Sauces with curious ingredients (swan sauce), memorable names (xo sauce) or multiple personalities (tartare sauce) merit attention here. Finally, new techniques from modernist cuisine have produced truly odd concoctions that challenge the very definition of sauce.

Dessert Sauces

A composed sauce served as part of a course to end the meal is still fairly rare in the spectrum of global cuisine, and the few examples are mainly European and North American. In French haute cuisine, dessert is the province of a separate kitchen (the *office*). Carême made this distinction clear: an elegant, artful dessert was the work of a *chef d'office habilé* but a well-executed menu demonstrated the 'scientific' prowess of a *chef de cuisine*.[1] Dessert sauces are often called 'crèmes', not sauces, and the most common French dessert sauce is a custard named crème anglaise, after the English preference for custards. La Varenne's '*crème d'Angleterre*' in *Le Cuisinier françois* (1651) was simply thickened, unsweetened cream but the French recipe developed into a thin egg custard over time. In response to the widespread use of the term crème anglaise for this sauce, Carême called his custards crèmes françaises in *Le Cuisinier parisien* (1828), taking a harder nationalist line with dessert sauce than he did with savoury sauces.

Crème Chantilly, sweetened whipped cream usually flavoured with vanilla, is persistently and erroneously attributed to François Vatel, maître d'hôtel to the Prince of Condé in the seventeenth century. The odd character of this sauce is tied to the desire to connect it to Louis xiv and the famous dinner given in honour of the king at the Château de Chantilly in 1671 that resulted in Vatel's suicide when the fish failed to arrive for the banquet. But Chantilly cream was not so named until the eighteenth century in Menon's *Les Soupers de la cour* (1755), in a recipe called *Fromage à la Chantilly glacé* for double cream whipped and flavoured with sugar and orange-flower water, set in a cheese mould.[2] Sweetened whipped cream called crème fouettée existed before Menon's recipe and French sources after Menon use crème fouettée and crème

Chantilly indiscriminately. Even Menon included a recipe for crème fouettée in the same cookbook, distinguished from the Chantilly recipe by the addition of an egg white or a stabilizing powder made from vetch. The association of Chantilly castle with the king, and by extension with fine food, gives this sauce a retroactive identity that is appealing and enduring, however false it may be.

One of the first uses of chocolate in French cooking was not in a dessert but a sauce for wigeon (a species of duck) – a chocolate ragoût from Massialot's cookbook of 1691. This recipe is curious for its early use of chocolate and for the information it offered that wigeon was suitable for Church-designated 'lean' days because it was classified as fish, not meat, owing to its perceived cold-bloodedness and its water habitat. Chocolate was a new commodity in late seventeenth-century France, and Massialot's instructions to 'make some chocolate' to add to the sauce do not help the modern reader much. Massialot also offered a recipe for a chocolate cream sauce with milk, egg yolk and sugar to be used 'wherever you like'.[3]

Oddly American

In the u.s., sweet sauces flavoured with chocolate, strawberry and butterscotch cover ice cream sundaes and other desserts. While chocolate sauce for dessert may not be odd and a number of commercial dessert sauces are sold in glass jars, the popularity of a chocolate sauce sold in a metal can is unusual. One of Milton S. Hershey's pet projects after the success of the Hershey company's manufacture of chocolate bars and cocoa powder, Hershey's chocolate syrup arrived in 1926 thanks to chief chemist Sam Hinkle.[4] It was first marketed to

Hershey's Syrup can, 1950s.

commercial users at soda fountains and ice cream parlours in two strengths: single (for carbonated drinks) and double (as a topping for ice cream). The product was immediately successful and was first sold for home use in late 1928, in cans for ease of serving and long shelf life. The Hershey factory in Pennsylvania already produced its own signature cans for cocoa powder, and soon thereafter installed machinery to turn out cans of Hershey's syrup on site. The chocolate sauce was sold exclusively in cans until 1979 when a plastic bottle was adopted, but the syrup is still available in 1 lb and 8 lb (450 g and 3.5 kg) cans. The canned syrup has its own set of fans, including survivalists and those who claim that the canned sauce tastes more like chocolate than the bottled version.

Cranberry sauce with roast turkey, the traditional American Thanksgiving meal.

Another now common but odd American sauce is the cranberry sauce served with turkey, mainly at Thanksgiving. The combination has historical justification, since the sweet, tart sauce served with savoury turkey recalls medieval dishes combining fruit and fowl, and the cranberry – native to New England – ties Americans to the site of the Pilgrims' arrival in the New World. Amelia Simmons first paired cranberry sauce with turkey in *American Cookery* (1796). Following the English taste for pickled condiments with roasted meats, her cookbook advised that stuffed roast turkey be served with cranberry sauce, mangoes, pickles or celery. Though no recipe was given, homemade cranberry sauce has relatively few ingredients and is simple to make. However, there is a notable preference in the u.s. for canned cranberry sauce. Commercial cranberry sauce originated in 1912 in Massachusetts with the

Cape Cod Cranberry Company, later to become Ocean Spray. If the flavour combination of meat with fruit is comprehensible, the practice of serving canned, jellied sauce in a fancy dish, with the outline of the can still visible on the quivering scarlet mass, is less so. The intrusion of an obviously commercial product on a festive table seems odd, but many American home-cooked Thanksgivings would be incomplete without the can of sauce.

As American as Thanksgiving, McDonald's has served its Big Mac hamburger with a 'special sauce' since 1968. The secret recipe was revealed in a video on the company's website in June 2012. Dan Coudreaut, an executive chef for McDonald's Canada, demonstrated how to make the Canadian Big Mac sauce at home with mayonnaise, pickle relish (chopped gherkins), mustard, white wine vinegar, garlic, onion powder and paprika.[5] The commercial recipe adds xanthan gum and some preservatives, and American Big Mac sauce contains high fructose corn syrup, caramel colour and a few more preservatives but is otherwise essentially the same.

Big Mac sauce from McDonald's, composed of mayonnaise, mustard, pickle relish and spices.

Buffalo chicken wings with hot pepper sauce.

Remarkably, Big Mac sauce does not contain ketchup, but two other regional American sauces with odd names have ketchup as a base: Utah 'fry sauce' (ketchup and mayonnaise), popular since the 1940s, and Mississippi 'comeback sauce' (ketchup, mayonnaise and chilli sauce), first served at Greek restaurants in Jackson, Mississippi, in the 1920s and now served on everything, including saltine crackers.

'Buffalo' chicken wings, with their pungent, bright red sauce, were invented in 1964 at the Anchor Bar in Buffalo, New York, by Teressa Bellissimo when she improvised a snack for her son and his friends with chicken wings, margarine and hot pepper sauce. Now Buffalo sauce appears on pizzas, sandwiches and burritos and every casual restaurant claims a proprietary recipe and a range of spiciness, from mild to incinerating. Mainly a mixture of vinegar, oil and hot spices, the sauce is hardly new. It fits squarely in the same category as *Apicius'* pepper-heavy sauces and brightly coloured medieval sharp sauces. The chicken wings are only a vehicle for the sauce and the hotter the better:

there is a daredevil quality to connoisseurs of the searing sauces. Eating challenges are common at restaurants known for the hottest wings, sauced with habanero peppers, 'ghost chillies' and quantities of cayenne. This is a sauce that often provokes more pain than pleasure, a suffering happily endured by countless willing patrons.

Odd Ingredients

The Middle Ages saw its share of odd sauces, but first among them might be the popular chawdron sauce, a British recipe served only with swan. The finished sauce was black, composed of swan innards boiled with blood, vinegar or wine and spices. A recipe in *The Forme of Cury* (1399) included liver, offal, bread crusts, swan blood, cloves and pepper. A showy sauce for those who could afford swan, the sauce remained in circulation through the seventeenth century. Robert May's 1660 recipe was definitive: 'Let your sauce be chaldron (sic) for a Swan, and serve it in saucers.'[6]

Not as curious as swan sauce but curious enough, American red-eye gravy is served with only one meat and has only two ingredients. It begins with Virginia (or Smithfield) ham cured with salt and smoked, a traditional practice in the American South since the mid-seventeenth century. A slice of country ham is fried in a hot skillet and boiling coffee completes the sauce; when the coffee combines with the fat from the ham, red 'eyes' form in the gravy. The legend that General (later President) Andrew Jackson's cook, red-eyed from a night of drinking, first prepared this sauce only further ties it to Southern cuisine and to Southern pride.

During the height of the ketchup craze in England, William Kitchiner published a recipe for 'Pudding Catsup'

Heinz Celery Sauce label from 1898, when celery sauce was a popular condiment in homes and restaurants in the U.S.

among the other recipes for savoury ketchups in *The Cook's Oracle* (1817). The sauce was composed of a half-pint of brandy or sherry steeped with cloves and mace for fourteen days, then combined with a pint of sugar syrup. Proposed as a tasty sauce for desserts when mixed with melted butter, Kitchiner claimed that this sauce would keep for years; the reader is inclined to believe him.

It seems odd now, but celery sauce was a common condiment sauce in the American nineteenth century, and one of the core products of the Heinz & Noble Company at the launch of their first commercial line in 1871. Before ketchup became their mainstay, the successor H. J. Heinz Company continued to manufacture celery sauce and promote it as a healthy food, since celery was believed to be good for brain and nerve function.[7] Homemade versions with boiled celery and cream appeared in a number of cookbooks, including Susannah Carter's *The Frugal Housewife* (1796) and Mary Randolph's *The Virginia Housewife* (1824). An accompaniment to roasted or boiled fowl, the condiment was a popular table sauce in restaurants in the U.S. until it fell out of favour in the early twentieth century.

Unclear Identity

Macaroni and cheese is a simple dish of pasta with cheese sauce, among the more prosaic of sauces. Yet its history ties it to both high and low cuisine and in its commercial form it is one of the oddest but most successful sauced dishes. Recipes for pasta cooked with cheese appeared as early as the fourteenth century in Europe in an elite context. But the true precursors of macaroni and cheese were recipes for pasta cooked in a milk and cheese sauce, either a roux-based white sauce (really a béchamel) or a custard-like mixture of milk and eggs. In the elegant food realm, Eliza Acton's 'Maccaroni à la Reine' in *Modern Cookery* (1868) offered an 'excellent and delicate mode of dressing maccaroni' using a sauce of rich cheese and a pint of cream, butter, mace and cayenne, virtually the same ingredients used today for homemade macaroni and cheese. Acton's recipe deliberately evoked elegance, from the writing style to the suggestion that a béchamel could be substituted for the white sauce or a portion of Stilton for the cheese.

Macaroni with a thick cheese sauce was embraced by American cuisine, especially in the American South and by African-American cooks, around the time of Randolph's recipe in *The Virginia Housewife* for 'Maccaroni Pudding': macaroni cooked with a mixture of eggs, cream and grated cheese. By 1896 Fannie Farmer's 'Baked Macaroni with Cheese' included a flour-and-butter white sauce and a buttered crumb topping. Today in its 'high' form the sauce might include lobster and fine cheeses, but it is equally at home at a church supper or a family dinner. The commercial version arrived in 1937 as 'Kraft Dinner', in a yellow box with shelf-stable grated cheese and dried pasta. Now in a blue box and with powdered cheese, the packaged sauce still seems to evoke its elegant forbears (with a little imagination) as the cook stirs in butter to *monter* the sauce of milk and orange powder. The product is called Kraft Macaroni and Cheese in the u.s. and Kraft Cheesey (sic) Pasta in the uk. Firmly in the realm of industrial food, Velveeta Shells and Cheese (introduced in 1984) includes a packet of semisolid cheese sauce that requires no milk or butter but does require a little faith that the orange mass will eventually melt into a sauce for the hot pasta.

Usually understood as a simple mayonnaise sauce for fried fish, tartare sauce has a surprising number of variations. In cookbooks from the nineteenth century onwards, tartare or tartar sauce is sometimes but not always the French sauce tartare (usually a mayonnaise with vinegar and herbs) and is occasionally something else entirely. Julia Child translated sauce tartare as 'Hard Yolk Mayonnaise' in *Mastering the Art of French Cooking*: hard-boiled egg yolks and mustard emulsified with oil, finished with minced pickles and capers. *Kettner's Book of the Table* calls tartare sauce 'the French idea of a devilled sauce', based as it was on either raw or hard egg yolks with mustard as the source of bedevilment.[8] Farmer offered both 'tartare sauce' and 'sauce tartare' in her cookbook. The former was nothing more than vinegar, lemon juice, Worcestershire sauce and browned butter; the latter was a raw-yolk mayonnaise with all of the expected ingredients plus powdered sugar and cayenne. And Charles Ranhofer in *The Epicurean* prepared 'Tartar Sauce' with velouté, mustard, fresh egg yolks, oil, vinegar, tarragon, chervil and chopped gherkins, but 'Tartar Sauce, English Style' (*sauce Tartare à l'Anglaise*) was hard-yolk mayonnaise done British-style with ground mustard, Harvey's sauce and Worcestershire.

Odd Names

Welsh rarebit (formerly rabbit) has nothing to do with rabbits and little to do with Wales. Another distinctly British sauce, early versions were simply melted cheese on toast but by the end of the nineteenth century Welsh rarebit was a liquid sauce made with mustard, beer or wine and melted cheese served over toast points. The term 'Welsh' was a patronizing label in the eighteenth century for a cheap substitute, and Welsh rabbit likely earned the name as a replacement for meat at simple suppers.[9] By 1865 the dish was called Welsh rarebit, although the transition to the more elegant term began in 1785 in a text that called the dish a 'rare bit'. What was once a humble, economical dish became an elegant supper dish in 1950s America, and Stouffer's still sells a frozen version made with cheddar cheese and Worcestershire sauce. The Welsh rarebit era may be ending, though, judging by the blunt question 'What is Welsh Rarebit?', asked and answered directly on the Stouffer's box.

A sauce that is (almost) a dish on its own, like Welsh rarebit, the Italian *bagna cauda* is an antipasto dish of anchovies and garlic simmered in butter and olive oil and eaten with raw

An advertisement for Ched-o-Bit cheese product to make Welsh rarebit, 1945.

vegetables. It has origins in Piedmont and suffers from an odd name (literally, 'hot bath') and an odd classification. It registers as a condiment or dipping sauce but for vegetables, but the sauce seems more important than the food it complements. *Bagna cauda* may be a relative of the ancient fish sauces, but raw vegetables were not part of the ancient diet. The name defies translation, and the sauce contains ingredients that are refused on principle by many eaters. Perhaps for this reason, the sauce has no real equivalent in other cuisines, except the Provençale *anchoïade* (anchovies, oil, garlic and vinegar) served at room temperature. *Bagna cauda* remains a hidden pleasure, far from the more common Italian sauces known the world over.

xo sauce was invented in Hong Kong in the 1980s and it has since become fantastically fashionable. In 2011, when *Vogue China* called it the 'caviar of the East', Lee Kum Kee sold a crystal bottle of xo sauce at auction for close to 7,000 yuan (over $1,000). The sauce is named for the highest grade of French cognac, but contains no cognac or brandy. Instead, its pricey ingredients make the name appropriate: dried scallops, shrimp and fish, Yunnan ham, garlic and chillies. Homemade versions keep indefinitely in the refrigerator, and commercial versions exist (such as Lee Kum Kee's, $31 for 8 oz/240 ml), but restaurants worldwide have jumped onto the trend with high-end dishes to match the sauce's reputation.

xo sauce on udon noodles, a simple dish to showcase an extravagant sauce.

Sauce chien from the French West Indies carries the off-putting name of 'dog sauce' when in reality it contains fairly mundane ingredients. The original version, probably from the nineteenth century, combined onions and acid (vinegar or lime juice) with scotch bonnet or habanero chillies plus pepper and garlic. More recent recipes use chopped tomatoes as well. A number of theories have been suggested to explain the name, all entertaining but none definitive: perhaps the most believable is that Chien was the brand of knife used by cooks preparing the ingredients for the sauce. Another sauce with an animal name, camel sauce from Middle Eastern cuisine, likewise contains no camel. A sweet and sour sauce with crushed almonds, it is coloured brown with cinnamon, and the name was perhaps a simple misspelling of the French word *cannelle*. It may also be related to the medieval cameline sauce made with cinnamon and other spices.

Is it a Sauce?

Hard sauce occupies two odd categories: as a dessert sauce and a sauce without a saucy consistency. Usually a creamy, stiff sauce used on steamed puddings, hard sauce is either 'hard' because of its texture or because it contains alcohol. It has a murky genealogy dating to the mid-nineteenth century, since the sauce is related to the stiff brandy and rum butters of England and to the 'Pudding Sauce' recipes made with wine found in British and American cookbooks, both in circulation at least since the eighteenth century. Still known as brandy butter in the UK, the thick mixture of butter, icing (confectioner's) sugar and brandy melts over warm puddings. The adjective 'hard' – meaning alcoholic – is an American colloquialism from the eighteenth century that might explain

Hard sauce (or brandy butter) with Christmas pudding.

the name for the sauce in the U.S., but early American recipes for 'hard sauce' similar to brandy butter contained no alcohol, as in Fannie Farmer's cookbook and Juliet Corson's textbook for the New York School of Cookery of 1877. These sauces used only butter and sugar and were chilled until firm: they were either puritanical revisions of brandy butter or literal translations of 'hard sauce' into a stiff, non-liquid sauce. Recipes for 'pudding sauce' in Kitchiner's British *Cook's Oracle* and *Miss Beecher's Domestic Receipt Book* (New York, 1846) called for butter, sugar and wine or brandy but were not 'hard' in name. Modern recipes nearly always include brandy, whiskey or cognac and are 'hard' in both senses.

Traditionally paired with game birds (or roast turkey or chicken), English bread sauce has few of the qualities expected of a gravy, lacking both the 'intrinsic gravy' of the roasted meat and a fluid consistency. The ancestor of bread sauce is frumenty, a fourteenth-century British porridge of boiled wheat, milk and egg yolks. Bread sauces may have grown out of the practice of thickening gravies with breadcrumbs

Bread sauce for poultry, claimed by some to be the British national sauce.

before roux became the liaison of choice. These sauces are still composed of bread, liquid and flavourings, and are midway between stuffing and sauce. In her eighteenth-century recipe Elizabeth Raffald soaked bread in water and boiled it in milk with onion, cloves, pepper and salt, adding butter and cream at the end. Later refinements exchanged boiled bread for boiled milk with flavourings and fresh breadcrumbs stirred into the milk. In an 1882 issue of *Household Words* edited by Charles Dickens, bread sauce was acclaimed as the British national sauce, a dubious honour considering that the author admitted it was often poorly made and that the French shunned British bread sauce, 'which they call by all sorts of unpleasant names, of which, indeed, it is for the most part highly deserving'.[10] Even Gordon Ramsay's present-day recipe replicates the elements of the original, ending with olive oil instead of butter but keeping the same flavourings and porridge-like texture. A classic British sauce by all accounts, bread sauce remains relatively true to its origins and perhaps in a class by itself.

At the furthest distance from the standard notion of sauce are the foams, ices and gels of modernist cuisine (or molecular gastronomy) and its chef adherents. Sauces have been transformed by the introduction of ingredients borrowed from chemistry labs and techniques informed by physicists, as chefs embrace the possibilities of new food forms that have led to a revision of food categories. Heston Blumenthal changed mustard from a condiment to a fanciful starter in 'pommery grain mustard ice cream with red cabbage gazpacho' at his Fat Duck restaurant outside London, guided by the chemical affinity between the two main ingredients (mustard and cabbage) and a desire to provoke the diner's senses. Wylie Dufresne conquered the physical qualities of liquid sauce with fried hollandaise, created for WD-50, his restaurant in New York. The dean of molecular gastronomy (even if he objects to the term) Ferran Adrià challenged and delighted his guests at the now closed El Bulli restaurant in Spain with spherified and reverse-spherified sauces, capsules and frozen elements, and dishes that required the diner to sauce his or her own plate. Grant Achatz and his team recently recreated some of El Bulli's most famous dishes, including smoke foam from 1997 and cauliflower couscous with solid herb sauce from 2000, at Next restaurant in Chicago, where Achatz's flagship restaurant Alinea is well known for cutting-edge molecular cuisine.

In the realm of elite cuisine, these sauces follow the philosophy (if not the technique) of the old school coulis, a tremendously expensive effort that results in a complex and exceptional product. Nathan Myhrvold opened the door to a wider audience with his monumental cookbooks *Modernist Cuisine* (2011) and *Modernist Cuisine at Home* (2012), demonstrating that this new approach to cooking is neither solely for restaurants nor about producing unrecognizable food. It is a means of perfecting cooking techniques, of better food through chemistry. Myrhvold's cookbooks have their share of astonishingly novel recipes, but *Modernist Cuisine at Home* applies its principles to simple dishes as well, like 'refined' macaroni and cheese. The recipe calls for sodium citrate, the same chemical used in processed cheese to keep the cheese from separating from the other ingredients in macaroni sauce. In Myhrvold's recipe it makes the creamy texture of industrial cheese sauce possible using fine cheeses. The result is high-end macaroni and cheese that looks for all the world as if it came out of a box, another melding of high and low and another disruption of food categories.

For sauces these methods overturn an already tentative classification. Sauce takes many forms but it is almost always a liquid. In modernist sauce a liquid state is no longer a requirement. Aerated foams created with liquid nitrogen and stabilized with lecithin perform the function of a sauce just as well as a gravy or a sauce Robert, if the goal is to complement the flavour of the main dish. Sauces have evolved from thick blankets to subtle juices to ethereal clouds and even

Foam sauce for venison by chef Grant Achatz at Alinea restaurant, Chicago.

Salad with spherified vinaigrette, an example of the influence of molecular gastronomy on sauce.

scented airs. They can be jellied, liquid inside a soft sphere or invisible while still being sauces. The old sauce masters have not been forgotten by the new guard: Myhrvold referenced 'the French sauce-making family tree' in his book,[11] and Next restaurant paid homage to Escoffier with its first themed dinner in 2011, 'Paris, 1906: Escoffier at the Ritz'. But Hervé This, who coined the now-disputed term 'molecular gastronomy' with Nicholas Kurti in 1992, departed entirely from these foundations in a curious recipe in *Kitchen Mysteries* (1993) for duck à l'orange that took an entirely new approach to sauce. This named the recipe *canard à la Brillat-Savarin* after the renowned nineteenth-century gastronome, placing it squarely in the French tradition even if the technique was far from traditional: duck thighs are fried in clarified butter to crisp the skin, injected with Cointreau and braised in the microwave.[12] The sauce is contained in the meat, present but invisible, the essence of modern cuisine.

6

Global Variations and National Identity

Certain sauces have clear national associations. *Mole* is, without question, Mexican, just as *nuoc mam* is Vietnamese and tomato ketchup belongs to the u.s., for example. The national identity of a sauce is sometimes direct, with a connection to the foods and food customs of that country, and sometimes circumstantial, a product of legend or an appropriation. Even sauces that bear a national identity in their name are not necessarily representative of that country or its cooking, especially if that name was imposed from the outside. Sauces associated with a certain cuisine or country may also carry metaphorical or political meaning. National sauce identities, like political identities, inspire both pride and defensiveness in the nations that bear them. This chapter examines the ways in which national sauces represent or misrepresent national cuisines as unique entities. Conversely, in spite of astounding worldwide variations in sauce, it is possible to identify a small number of 'master sauces' that span the globe.

Sauces named for the places they represent are a useful starting point for a study of national sauce identity, but these names are not wholly reliable. As previously mentioned, sauce espagnole or 'Spanish sauce', the French mother sauce, recognizes seventeenth-century Spanish cooks brought to France with the royal bride of Louis xiv but the sauce itself does not evoke Spanish cuisine, except the technique of cooking flour to a nut-brown colour (hardly limited to Spanish cooking) and the use of ham as the basis for the essential coulis. Antonio Latini in *Lo scalco alla moderna* (1692) used the term 'alla spagnuola' (Spanish-style) not for sauce espagnole but to designate tomato sauce recipes, because Spanish traders helped to introduce this fruit into continental cuisine. Neither espagnole nor tomato sauce dominates Spanish cuisine today, but *allioli* (aïoli, garlic and olive oil mayonnaise) has been called the national sauce of Catalonia by José Andrés, among others. As late as the mid-nineteenth century, so-called 'Italian' sauce in French and British cookbooks contained mushrooms, shallots, parsley and espagnole or velouté, but no tomatoes.[1] Hannah Glasse offered 'Cullis the Italian Way' in 1747 with ham, gravy, basil and mushrooms. Since the nineteenth century, sauces labelled *alla Napoletana* usually contain tomatoes, and the assigned national sauce for Italy by those outside the country is tomato sauce, although it is not called 'Italian sauce'. The only composed sauce named for America has a weak claim to the term: lobster with sauce *à l'Américaine* with tomatoes and white wine may have been named for America by a French chef who worked in Chicago or it may be a misspelling of 'Armoricaine', from Armor, the ancient name for the Brittany coast.

A number of sauces named after nations originated in the French system, following the French compulsion for naming their creations and indicative of Carême's conviction that French sauces were the gold standard, superior to those of Russia, England, Germany and Italy. In fact, Carême declared, the French appropriated and perfected these countries' sauces; their French names were only logical. English cookbooks calling for Dutch (hollandaise), Spanish or German sauces on the French model further cemented these labels, accurate or not. Some of the Frenchified sauces in Escoffier and the *Répertoire de la cuisine* correspond vaguely to the cuisines evoked by their names: sauce italienne has a base of demi-glace and tomatoes; sauce russe contains mayonnaise, lobster tomalley and caviar; and Oxford sauce is a variation on Cumberland sauce, a classic British sauce of redcurrant jelly and orange peel. But these designations are nevertheless external, based on the French perception of the respective cuisines.

Class plays a role in the dominance of French sauces, of course. Condiment sauces generally retain their regional or national character because they belong to the middle and lower classes who tend to eat where they live, from local and economically accessible products. The upper classes, then as now, seek to demonstrate their ability to eat how and what they please. If swan is the most prestigious meat, swan will be had and where there is swan there is chawdron sauce. French sauces have an established reputation as the best cuisine has to offer, and elite diners all over the world indulge in French dishes with French names on the menu, no matter whether the national language is English, Russian or Japanese. In arguments about the globalization and homogenization of food, it is not ketchup that should win the title of world sauce but the gilded French sauces, the ones that provoked a social revolution in 1789 (metaphorically, of course, as representative of royal excess, but 'Let them eat velouté!' would have done the trick) and a culinary revolution in 1973 with nouvelle cuisine, but that continue to circle the world.

In light of the French influence, self-imposed national sauce names might be more reliable as representations of culinary identity. Carême's sauce à la française in *L'Art de la cuisine française* (1833) had French ingredients (béchamel and

Hollandaise or Dutch sauce, which is French in spite of its name.

mushroom essence, finished with crawfish butter), made even more French in *The Epicurean* (1894) with the addition of demi-glace. Cavalcanti's *salsa all'Italiana* in *Cucina teorico-pratica* (1837) was made with mushrooms, onion, white wine and the master sauce here called *sugo colato* (strained sauce). But because Italian cuisine cannot be reduced to one sauce, Cavalcanti accounted for regional identities with *maccheroni alla Siciliana* – made of aubergine (eggplant), *buon sugo* (good sauce) and grated cheese – and in 1891 Artusi confirmed *maccheroni alla Napoletana* and *alla Bolognese* as equally Italian sauces. Mexican tomato and chilli sauce is *salsa mexicana* in Mexico, and 'English sauce' in many nineteenth-century British cookbooks is melted butter sauce, except for those

Tomato salsa with tortilla chips, also known as *salsa mexicana* or *pico de gallo*.

that give bread sauce the national honour. Eliza Acton in *Modern Cookery* resignedly admitted that even foreigners called butter sauce 'the one sauce of England'.[2]

Or perhaps the truest national sauces are those with a name that simply means 'sauce'. For China, *chiang* and its modifiers fit the bill, especially soy sauce or *chiang yu*, which has had a profound influence on Chinese cuisine and on linguistic forms for other sauces. Soy sauce is fundamental to Chinese and Japanese cooking, as are the many varieties of salsa (sauce) in Mexico, and *mole poblano*, the complex dish named for *molli* or sauce. After tomato ketchup was established in the UK, commercial competitors like HP, O.K. and Flag introduced products that were so common on British tables that they were 'often simply known as "sauce"'.[3]

Vinegary sauces like HP and O.K. are more popular in the UK than anywhere else, and are affectionately acknowledged as uniquely British. Kitchiner's term 'intrinsic gravy' defined another British sauce – meat gravy – in an elemental way: it is a sauce from and for meat. On the other hand, the complexity of French cuisine is demonstrated by multiple base terms for sauce, among them jus, coulis, fonds and essence.

An association between a sauce and a national cuisine may be determined by local ingredients or practices. It makes sense that *nuoc-mam*, a preserved-fish sauce, dominates the cuisine of Vietnam as the country is surrounded by water and has a fish-heavy diet. The popularity of spicy sauces in Spain can be explained by the agricultural presence of the chilli pepper there as early as 1493, making Spaniards and the Portuguese the first Europeans to use chillies in cooking. Jean-Robert Pitte asserted that French sauce is superior to all others because French wines, a primary ingredient, are superior.[4] Americans were receptive to scientific claims about nutrition and food safety in the nineteenth century, adopting commercial bottled sauces (ketchup among them) after companies touted the purity and health benefits of factory-made sauces. Americans also appreciate efficiency, manifest in condiment sauces for food on the go and sauces that replace vegetables on a school lunch tray. Ketchup was rejected as a substitute for vegetables in federally funded school lunches during the Reagan era, but salsa earned the endorsement of the U.S. Department of Agriculture during the Clinton administration.[5] America may be the land of pioneers, but in terms of sauce the U.S. plays it conservative. Ketchup is always tomato and usually from Heinz, gravy is fine from a can, and mustard is mild and bright yellow. Then again, modernist sauce in high-end restaurants has its largest audience in the U.S., meaning that conservative sauce underpinnings still leave room for liberal movement in the upper tier.

Circumstances and customs play a role in establishing national sauces as well. According to Elizabeth David, the British transferred the medieval practice of consuming quantities of imported spices on meats or in ragoûts to heavily spiced ketchups, vinegars and mustards that became popular in the eighteenth century. Colin Spencer ties these strong sauces to masculinity, claiming that Beeton's pungent sauces cast aside Victorian timidity and that 'the menfolk would obviously insist on having powerful sauces and pickles, especially when out subjugating the natives in the colonies.'[6] The existence of a national cuisine in Italy remains a matter of debate, even for Italians. Italy, was unified in 1861, significantly later than its European neighbours. As a result, regional cooking continues to thrive and no definitive national sauce exists in Italy despite outsiders' efforts to claim that tomato sauce is the one sauce of Italy, and despite the success of Italian-American tomato gravy in its New World home. However, there is an identifiably Italian sauce practice: the 'condimento' rule for pasta sauce that dresses pasta without drowning it, a reflection of the Italian internalization of food scarcity following numerous periods of economic instability.

In terms of national sauce practices, Japanese sauces privilege aesthetics; these light broths or glazes do not cover food but highlight it. To maintain the colour and texture of carefully chosen and sliced fish in sashimi, for example, the sushi chef may brush on a small amount of transparent sauce. Prepared Japanese sauces contain few ingredients, usually transparent liquids. Ponzu sauce for very thinly sliced raw fish combines soy sauce and vinegar with *yuzu* (a citrus fruit) juice and *mirin* (sweet rice wine), for example. A heavy covering of sauce would be counterintuitive in dishes that emphasize the quality and inherent beauty of the main ingredient. Thick British gravy, on the other hand, is meant to blanket. It is

Menu of Italian regional specialities for a banquet held by Italian citizens in Nice, France, in 1888.

Sashimi with wasabi and soy sauce.

merely a coincidence that in the seventeenth century Menon called his sauce à l'Anglaise (English sauce) especially good 'to cover dishes that do not look very nice', since the recipe predated the age of floury gravy in British cuisine, but the sentiment was oddly appropriate.[7] Gravy remains part of the family meal in British cuisine, still thick and comforting but more complement than distraction.

Intimations of national tendencies in cuisine and especially in sauce occasionally lead to defensiveness by partisans of that cuisine. The British are justly proud of their native table sauces (that are, truth be told, adapted from Indian sauces) but defensive about the fact that their cuisine is second to France and therefore that their fine sauces are French imports. Eneas Sweetland Dallas responded to mockery of the one English sauce (melted butter) by saying that French cooking 'with all its pretensions, ought to be ashamed of the monotony produced by aspic'.[8] Not exactly the shot heard round the world, but the French are no more heroic: certain as they are of their superiority in sauce, they still take pains to defend it. The practice of naming sauces adds to the dominance of French sauce; in no other cuisine do fundamental sauces branch out into a tree of rigidly defined preparations. Yet the *Répertoire de la cuisine* warned that giving a new name to a well-known dish or calling a new dish by a well-known name are 'bad practices' that 'will debase the culinary art beyond redemption'.[9] Tavenet, the champion of French sauce names, protested the names 'sauce espagnole' and 'sauce allemande' specifically because they made the French seem weak 'in a discipline that declares itself to be so eminently French'.[10] To make the point that national differences in cooking techniques still exist, Flandrin and Montanari asserted that 'the art of the sauce, which is all but unknown or mis-applied in many European countries, continues to flourish in France and Belgium.'[11]

In Mexico and Italy, sauces have been drawn into politics and appeals to nationalism. Called the national sauce of Mexico by some, *mole* performs a balancing act as representative of Creole and colonial cooking. It contains a mix of indigenous and European ingredients and is inscribed in legends that testify to or erase native culinary ingenuity, depending on the reader. But the most ardent defensive refrain about *mole* is that it is not 'chocolate sauce' nor 'chocolate chicken', as its champions fear it will be known. *Mole* aficionados and recipe authors insist that the dish contains only a very small quantity of chocolate, as if to rescue the sauce from further alienation as an incomprehensible product.

During Benito Mussolini's fascist regime in Italy, the Futurist Filippo Marinetti made an overt connection between food and nationalism in *Cucina futurista* (1932). His effort to revise the Italian culinary identity related to pasta, the vehicle for sauce, was part of his call for an Italian national identity that would be supported and maintained by the state. Marinetti condemned pasta because it was nutritionally inferior to meat, because it caused Italy to be dependent on foreign wheat and because the pervasive image of the *mangiamaccheroni* eating pasta with their hands encouraged the idea that Italians were unsophisticated 'in contrast with the lively spirit and the passionate, generous, intuitive soul of Neapolitans'.[12] Tomato sauce remained Italian, however, in a recipe called 'Mare d'Italia' (Italian Sea): lines of fresh tomato sauce and spinach purée with pieces of fish, banana, cherry and fig. Marinetti's cookbook called for new flavour combinations, rejected the insidious influence of the past and emphasized the sensory experience of flavours, perfumes and colours in food presentation. The dish 'Rombi d'ascesa' (Roars of Ascent) correctly applied the new sauce philosophy, accenting white risotto with *salsa luminosa* (veal stock with

The ingredients for *mole poblano* in order of importance: fresh and dried chillies, nuts, seeds, tomatoes, aromatics and a bit of chocolate in the background.

marsala, rum and orange) and store-bought *salsa nazionale*. Although Marinetti's recipes are occasionally recreated by culinary artists, interest in Futurist Italian cooking was short-lived and ultimately unable to unseat pasta with sauce as one of Italy's national foods.

Most countries have national sauce traditions and sauces can distinguish one cuisine from another on the local level. Given a global perspective, however, it is possible to identify the common ancestors of these individual sauces and reduce them to four transcontinental 'master sauces'. Vinegar, the foundational sauce ingredient that pre-dates even fish and soy sauce, was essential to the *poivrade* sauces and sauce Robert common to western Europe. With the addition of meat juices, these early models led to the more complex French sauces. Vinegar also ties together northern Europe's mustard countries, tomato ketchup in the u.s., Latin America's *escabeche* and *chimichurri*, the Argentine national sauce of garlic, herbs and vinegar. The mayonnaise zone is more localized, extending from Belgian chip shops to Holland, the namesake of hollandaise sauce, to Spain and aïoli country, to *avgolemono* (lemon, egg and meat stock) sauce in Greece. Mayonnaise has a foothold as a secondary sauce in Japan and Russia as well. The spicy 'red revolution' family of sauces has branches on at least three continents: harissa in North Africa, *mole* in Mexico and Tabasco in the southern u.s., from which any number of cousins are scattered across the world, including tomato-based salsas and pasta sauces. Finally, fermented sauces have the deepest history and the widest coverage of all sauces, encompassing Chinese and Japanese soy, the fish sauces of Southeast Asia, Greek and Roman *garum*, pungent Indian sauces that inspired British walnut ketchups and Worcestershire, and ultimately all the sauces that add an almost indescribable *umami* flavour to food.

Greek *avgolemono* sauce served over chicken. *Avgolemono* is a member of the mayonnaise family of sauces.

It seems fitting to end this history of sauce with the word *umami* because the term aligns particularly well with sauce as an abstract and a material concept. If a single characteristic is common to all sauces, it is the role of sauce as an accent, a secondary player, the harmony to the main ingredient's melody. The flavour that sauce adds should be indefinable, almost beyond description, in the way that the word *umami* approximates but does not fully explain the idea of savoury meatiness that it is meant to convey. Any attempt to put into words the flavour of Worcestershire Sauce, say, or béchamel, will fail for lack of adequate adjectives. Sauce may be complex, the result of many steps and practised techniques, but its complexity should be subtle, discreet and indecipherable. Simple sauces are inherently subtle and are never as simple as they seem. Often the result of a process that demands time and patience, that requires science or art or both, sauce can be inscrutable. Why do rotten fish make food taste better? What is the secret to mayonnaise? What *is* that flavour in the sauce? And this is the key to its longevity: open to endless variation, sauce will continue to fuel the creativity of chefs and diners on tables high and low. The future of sauce is assured. Unnecessary but essential, sauce is here to stay.

Recipes

Historical Recipes

Macreuse en ragout au chocolat
—from François Massialot, *Le Cuisinier royal et bourgeois* (1691)

Having properly plucked and cleaned your wigeon, empty and clean it; blanch it on the fire and then pot it, seasoning it with salt, pepper, bay, and a bundle of herbs. Make a little chocolate to toss it in. Meanwhile, prepare a ragoût with the liver, mushrooms, morels, meadow mushrooms, truffles, a quarter of a pound of chestnuts, and your wigeon now cooked and laid out on a platter. Serve your ragout over the wigeon, and garnish it as you like.

Tomato Sauce, Spanish Style
—from Antonio Latini, *Lo scalco alla moderna* (1692),
translation by Rudolf Grewe

Take half a dozen tomatoes that are ripe, and put them to roast in the embers, and when they are scorched, remove the skin diligently, and mince them finely with a knife. Add onions, minced finely, to discretion; hot chili peppers, also minced finely; and thyme in a small amount. After mixing everything together, adjust it with a little salt, oil, and vinegar. It is a very tasty sauce, both for boiled dishes or anything else.

Timbale of Vermicelli with Tomatoes
(Neapolitan Receipt)
—from Antonia Isola (Mabel Earl McGinnis), 1912, borrowed from
Ippolito Cavalcanti, 1837

Take ten medium-sized fresh tomatoes and cut them in two cross-
wise. Put a layer of these into a baking dish with the liquid side
touching the bottom of the dish. Now put another layer with the
liquid side up, sprinkle on salt and pepper. Break the raw vermicelli
the length of the baking dish and put a layer of it on top of the
tomatoes. Now add another layer of the tomatoes with the skin side
touching the vermicelli, a second layer with the liquid side up, salt and
pepper, and another layer of the raw vermicelli, and so on, the top
layer being of tomatoes with their liquid side touching the vermicelli.
Heat three or four tablespoons of good lard (or butter), and when
the lard boils pour it over the tomatoes and vermicelli; then put the
dish into the oven and cook until the vermicelli is thoroughly done.
After cooling a little while, turn it out into a platter.

Mushroom Catsup
—from William Kitchiner, *The Cook's Oracle* (1822)

Look out for Mushrooms from the beginning of September.
Take care they are the right sort, and *fresh gathered*. Full grown
Flaps are to be preferred: put a layer of these at the bottom of a
deep earthen pan, and sprinkle them with salt, and then another
layer of mushrooms; let them remain two or three hours, by
which time the salt will have penetrated the mushrooms, and rendered them easy to break. Then pound them in a mortar, or mash
them well with your hands, and let them remain for a couple of
days, not longer, stirring them up, and mashing them well each
day. Then pour them into a stone jar, and to each quart add an
ounce of whole black pepper. Stop the jar very close and set it in
a stewpan of boiling water, and keep it boiling for two hours at
least. Take out the jar, and pour the juice clear from the settlings

through a hair sieve (without squeezing* the mushrooms) into a clean stew[pan]; let it boil very gently for half an hour. Those who are for Superlative Catsup will continue the boiling till the mushroom juice is reduced to half the quantity. It may then be called *Double Cat*-sup or Dog-sup . . . Pour it into a clean dry jar or jug; cover it close and let it stand in a cool place till next day, then pour it off as gently as possible (so as not to disturb the settlings at the bottom of the jug) through a tammis or thick flannel bag, till it is perfectly clear. Add a tablespoonful of good Brandy to each pint of Catsup, and let it stand as before; a fresh sediment will be deposited, from which the Catsup is to be quietly poured off and bottled in pints or half pints (which have been washed with Brandy or spirit). It is best to keep it in such quantities as are soon used.

* The squeezings are the perquisite of the Cook, to make sauce for the second table. Do not deprive her of it, it is the most profitable save-all you can give her, and will enable her to make up a good family dinner with what would otherwise be wasted. After the mushrooms have been squeezed, dry them in the Dutch oven and make mushroom powder.

To Make a Gravy for a Turkey, or Any Sort of Fowls
—from Hannah Glasse, *The Art of Cookery* (1747)

Take a pound of the lean part of the beef, hack it with a knife, flour it well, have ready a stew-pan with a piece of fresh butter. When the butter is melted put in the beef, fry it till it is brown, and then pour in a little boiling water. Stir it altogether, and put in two or three blades of mace, four or five cloves, some whole pepper, an onion, a bundle of sweet herbs, a little crust of bread baked brown, and a little piece of carrot. Cover it close, and let it stew till it is as good as you would have it. This will make a pint of rich gravy.

French Sauce (*Sauce à la française*)
—from Charles Ranhofer, *The Epicurean* (1894)

Reduce one pint of béchamel with two gills of mushroom essence in a saucepan, season with mignonette and nutmeg and half a small clove of crushed and chopped garlic, as well as a tablespoonful of meat glaze. Just when ready to serve incorporate into the sauce four ounces of crawfish butter, strain through a tammy, then add a teaspoonful of vinegar and chopped parsley.

Maccaroni à La Reine
—from Eliza Acton, *Modern Cookery* (1868)

This is a very excellent and delicate mode of dressing maccaroni. Boil eight ounces in the usual way, and by the time it is sufficiently tender, dissolve gently ten ounces of any rich, well flavoured white cheese in full three-quarters of a pint of good cream; add a little salt, a rather full seasoning of cayenne, from half to a whole salt-spoonful of pounded mace, and a couple of ounces of sweet fresh butter. The cheese should, in the first instance, be sliced very thin, and taken quite free of the hard part adjoining the rind; it should be stirred into the cream without intermission until it is entirely dissolved, and the whole is perfectly smooth: the maccaroni, previously well drained, may then be tossed gently in it, or after it is dished, the cheese may be poured equally over the maccaroni. The whole, in either case, may be thickly covered before it is sent to table, with fine crumbs of bread fried of a pale gold colour, and dried perfectly, either before the fire or in an oven, when such an addition is considered an improvement. As a matter of precaution, it is better to boil the cream before the cheese is melted in it; rich white sauce, or *béchamel*, made not very thick, with an additional ounce or two of butter, may be used to vary and enrich this preparation. If Parmesan cheese be used for it, it must of course be grated; but as we have said before, it will not easily blend with the other ingredients so as to be smooth. A portion of

Stilton, free from the blue mould, would have a good effect in the present receipt. Half the quantity may be served.

Maccaroni, ½ lb; cheese, 10 oz.; good cream, ¾ pint (or rich white sauce); butter, 2 oz. (or more); little salt, *fine* cayenne, and mace.

Sauce Robert Five Ways

Longe de porc a la sauce Robert (Pork Loin with Sauce Robert)
—from Pierre François La Varenne, *Le Cuisinier françois* (1651)

Lard the meat with pork fat, then roast it, and baste it with verjuice and vinegar and a bouquet of sage. When the fat has rendered, use it to fry an onion, which once fried you will put under the loin with the sauce from basting. When the dish has simmered together a bit, being careful not to let it harden, serve. This sauce is called sauce Robert.

Salsa Roberta
—from Vincenzo Corrado, *Il cuoco galante* (1773)

Lightly cook the onions, well minced, with butter, and combine with minced small capers, coriander, and spices, boil in Muscat wine and bitter lemon, and serve the sauce.

Sauce à la Robert
—from Marie-Antonin Carême, *L'Art de la cuisine française au XIXe siècle* (1833)

After having cut three large onions in small dice, brown them lightly in clarified butter, then drain them and simmer them with consommé and two large spoonfuls of simmered Espagnole.

When the sauce is perfectly reduced, mix in a little powdered sugar, a little pepper, a little vinegar, and a teaspoon of fine mustard.

Robert Sauce
—from Louis Diat, *Sauces, French and Famous* (1951)

1 tbsp butter
2 tbsp finely chopped onions
1 glass (3 oz) white wine
1 tbsp vinegar
1 cup brown sauce
2 tbsp tomato sauce or tomato purée
1 tsp prepared mustard
1 tbsp finely chopped sour pickles
1 tsp chopped parsley

Melt butter in saucepan, add onions and cook until they are golden brown. Add wine and vinegar and cook until reduced to three-fourths the original quantity. Add brown and tomato sauces and cook slowly 10–15 minutes. When ready to serve, add mustard, pickles, and chopped parsley. Used for pork, pork chops, and leftover meat.

Sauce Robert (Brown Mustard Sauce)
—from Julia Child, Simone Beck and Louisette Bertholle,
Mastering the Art of French Cooking (1961)

For: roast or braised pork, pork chops, boiled beef, broiled chicken, turkey, hot meat leftovers, hamburgers.

a heavy-bottomed 6-cup saucepan or your meat-cooking pan
with its degreased juices
¼ cup finely minced yellow onions
1 tbsp butter
1 tsp oil or cooking fat

1 cup dry white wine or ⅔ cup dry vermouth
2 cups brown sauce
3 to 4 tbsp Dijon-type prepared mustard creamed with 2 to 3
tbsp softened butter and ⅛ tsp sugar
2 to 3 tbsp fresh minced parsley

Cook the onions slowly with the butter and oil or fat for 10 to 15 minutes until they are tender and lightly browned. Add the wine and boil it down rapidly until it is reduced to 3 or 4 tablespoons. Add the brown sauce and simmer 10 minutes. Correct seasoning. Off heat and just before serving, beat the mustard mixture into the sauce, tasting. Beat in the parsley and serve.

Modern Recipes

Sauce espagnole
—from Auguste Escoffier, *Le Guide culinaire* (1921)

Proportions for 5 litres:
roux for binding: 626 g
brown fonds for the entire sauce recipe: 12 litres
mirepoix, for aromatic base: 150 g of pork belly finely diced;
250 g of carrot and 150 g of onion cut in large brunoise;
2 bundles of thyme; 2 small bay leaves.

Procedure:
1. Put 8 litres of fonds on the boil; add the roux, softened in advance; mix with a spatula or a whisk and bring the sauce to the boil while stirring. Keep it warm on the side of the fire, at a slow and regular boil.
2. Add the mirepoix prepared thus: Melt the lard in a saucepan; toss in the brunoise of carrot and onion, thyme and bay, sauté this until the vegetables are lightly browned. Then carefully skim off the fat; put the vegetables in the sauce; then deglaze the saucepan with a glass of white wine. Reduce by half; add this

deglazed liquid also to the sauce and let it cook slowly for one hour, skimming it frequently to remove the scum.

3. Pour the sauce into a chinois or into another dish, pressing lightly on the mirepoix; moisten it again with 2 litres of fonds; allow another 2 hours of slow and careful boiling. Finally, pour the sauce into a terrine and swirl it in the pan until it has cooled completely.

4. The next day, put the sauce back into a heavy-bottomed casserole, with: 2 litres of fonds, a litre of puréed tomatoes or the equivalent amount of fresh tomatoes, about 2 kilos. If using purée, we suggest that you put it in the oven until it has taken on a light brown colour, in order to cut the acidity. Thus prepared, the tomato facilitates the clarification of the sauce, at the same time as it gives the sauce a warmer tone that is more pleasing to the eye. Bring the sauce to a boil on high heat, stirring it with a spatula or whisk; keep it at a slow boil for one hour and finish removing the remaining scum during this time with the highest degree of attention. Pass it through a tamis and swirl it until it has cooled completely.

Canard à la Brillat-Savarin
—from Hervé This, *Kitchen Mysteries* (2007),
translation by Jody Gladding

Begin with thighs that you have grilled in clarified butter over a very hot flame but for a very short time, long enough to allow a lovely golden crust to appear. The clarification of butter, that is, melting butter slowly and using only the liquid fatty portion of the melted product, is useful as butter thus treated does not darken during cooking. After the first grilling process, the meat is still inedible because the center remains raw, and we know that duck must be cooked! Using a paper towel, blot the fat from the surface of the thighs, and, using a syringe, inject the center of the meat with Cointreau (better yet, with Cointreau into which you have dissolved salt and infused pepper). Place the thighs in a microwave for a few minutes (the precise amount of time will vary according to the number of pieces and the power of the oven). During the cooking process, the surface of the meat will dry slightly and need no further treatment. On the other hand, the center of the meat will be 'braised' in an alcohol vapor and flavored with orange (my own personal taste also prompts me to stud the flesh with cloves before microwaving it).

Spare yourself the trouble of making a sauce: it is already in the meat. No need to flambé; the alcohol has already permeated the flesh. Check your watch: you will see that putting science to work has cost you no time; quite the contrary. Furthermore, it has rejuvenated an old recipe by making it lighter.

References

1 The Origin and Conception of Sauce

The epigraph comes from Bénigne Poissenot, *L'Esté* [1583] in *Conteurs français du XVIe siècle*, ed. Pierre Jourda (Paris, 1956) p. 1308. Unless otherwise indicated, all translations from French and Italian sources are my own.

1 H. T. Huang and Joseph Needham, *Science and Civilization in China*, vol. VI, part 5 of *Fermentations and Food Science* (Cambridge, 2000), p. 334.
2 Ibid., p. 358.
3 See studies by Y. Sumiyoshi (1986) and Wang Shan-Tien (1987) cited ibid., p. 377.
4 Ibid., p. 392.
5 Naomichi Ishige, 'Cultural Aspects of Fermented Fish Products in Asia', in *Fish Fermentation Technology*, ed. Cheri-Ho Lee, Keith H. Steinkraus and P. J. Alan Reilly (Tokyo, 1993), p. 23.
6 Pliny the Elder, *The Natural History*, ed. and trans. John Bostock and H. T. Riley (London, 1855), book 9, chap. 30.
7 The cookbook named *Apicius* is a compilation of recipes from the first century AD to at least the fourth or fifth and possibly later, with revisions and additions along the way. The two extant manuscripts date to the ninth century.
8 Christopher Grocock and Sally Grainger, eds, *Apicius:*

A Critical Edition (London, 2006), pp. 375–86.

9 M.F.K. Fisher, 'An Alphabet for Gourmets' [1949], in *The Art of Eating* (Hoboken, NJ, 2004), pp. 643–4.

10 Quoted in Huang, *Science and Civilization*, p. 354.

11 Ken Albala, *Eating Right in the Renaissance* (Berkeley, CA, 2002), pp. 253–4.

12 Grocock and Grainger, *Apicius*, recipe 1.11.

2 Condiment Sauces

1 M. Tullius Cicero, *De finibus bonorum et malorum* (*On the Limits of Good and Evil*), book 2 section 90. Modern edition ed. Thomas Schiche (Leipzig, 1915). Cicero is quoting Socrates in this passage; the usual English translation is 'Hunger is the best sauce.'

2 'Non son vivande, ma sebbene condimenti, che furono a bella posta inventati, e nelle mense imbanditi, o per dar maggior condimento ad una qualche vivanda, o per avvalorare qualche stomaco rilasciato, o pure per titillare le papille a quel palato.' Vincenzo Corrado, *Il cuoco galante* [1773], 2nd edn (Naples, 1793), p. 141.

3 Andrew Smith, 'Ketchup', in *Oxford Companion to American Food and Drink*, ed. Andrew Smith (Oxford, 2007), p. 342.

4 Elizabeth Raffald, *The Experienced English Housekeeper* (Manchester, 1769), p. 318.

5 Paul von Bergen quoted in Poppy Brech, 'Brand Health Check: Heinz Ketchup', *Marketing Magazine*, 20 July 2000.

6 Andrew Smith, 'Mayonnaise', in *Oxford Companion to American Food and Drink*, ed. Smith, p. 370.

7 '*Lazenby v. White*. November 18, 1870', *Law Journal Reports*, XLI (1872), p. 354.

8 Lizzie Collingham, *Curry: A Tale of Cooks and Conquerors* (Oxford, 2006), p. 149.

9 Buwei Yang Chao, *How to Cook and Eat in Chinese* (New York, 1945), p. 29.

10 'Outline of the H. J. Heinz Company', MSS 57, box 2, folder

7, Historical Society of Western Pennsylvania, p. 2. Quoted in Nancy F. Koehn, *Brand New: How Entrepreneurs Earned Consumers' Trust from Wedgwood to Dell* (Boston, MA, 2001), p. 58 n. 77. With the addition of a third partner, the company was renamed Heinz, Noble & Company in 1872.

11 Bartolomeo Scappi, *The Opera of Bartolomeo Scappi* [1570], trans. and ed. Terence Scully (Toronto, 2008), vol. II, p. 276.

12 Ippolito Cavalcanti, *Cucina teorico-pratica*, 2nd edn (Naples, 1839), p. 254.

13 J. W. Courter and A. M. Rhodes, 'Historical Notes on Horseradish', *Economic Botany*, XXIII/2 (1969), pp. 156–64.

14 David Sprinkle of Packaged Facts quoted in Judy Hevrdejs, 'Goin' for the Burn: Old-timer Tabasco vs. Hip Sriracha in Hot Sauce Smackdown', *Chicago Tribune*, 10 October 2010.

15 'Company Information', Huy Fong Foods Inc. website, www.huyfong.com, accessed 31 May 2011.

16 Bernard Rosenberger, 'Arab Cuisine and its Contribution to European Culture', in *Food: A Culinary History*, ed. Albert Sonnenfeld (New York, 1999), pp. 215–20.

17 The term *pico de gallo* is not found in the *Diccionario de la lengua española* of the Real Academia Española, 22nd edn (Madrid, 2001). In the *Diccionario Breve de Mexicanismos* (Mexico City, 2001) it is defined as a sauce of prickly pear, onion and chillies.

18 Florence Fabricant, 'Riding Salsa's Coast-to-coast Wave of Popularity', *New York Times*, 2 June 1993.

19 Andre Mouchard, 'Hasta la vista, Ketchup! Sales of Salsa and other Mexican Sauces', *Orange County Register*, 30 May 1993.

20 NPD Group market research survey cited in 'Ketchup is Still King in Battle with Hot Salsa', *Pittsburgh Observer-Reporter*, 9 August 1994.

21 Arlene Davila, *Latinos, Inc.: The Marketing and Making of a People* (Berkeley, CA, 2012), pp. 54–5.

22 Robert A. Underwood, 'Dear Colleague' letter to the Congress of the United States, 'The Ketchup-only Bill: Our National Condiment!', 18 October 1995.

3 French Sauces

1 'Les sauces sont la parure et l'honneur de la cuisine française; elles ont contribué à lui procurer et à lui assurer cette supériorité.' *Larousse gastronomique* (Paris, 2000), p. 2176.

2 'Les sauces représentent la partie capitale de la cuisine. Ce sont elles qui ont créé et maintenu l'universelle prépondérance de la cuisine française.' Auguste Escoffier, *Le Guide culinaire* (Paris, 1993), p. 4.

3 'C'est justement comme un homme qui aurait trouvé une sauce excellente, et qui voudrait examiner si elle est bonne sur les préceptes du *Cuisinier français*.' Molière, *La Critique de l'École des femmes* [1663], Act 1, scene 6, in *Oeuvres complètes*, ed. Pierre-Aimé Touchard (Paris, 1962).

4 Jean-Robert Pitte, *Gastronomie française: Histoire et géographie d'une passion* (Paris, 1991), p. 130.

5 Julia Child, Simone Beck and Louisette Bertholle, *Mastering the Art of French Cooking* (New York, 1961), p. 58.

6 Louis-Eustache Ude, *The French Cook; or, the Art of Cookery*, 3rd edn (London, 1815), p. 10.

7 Child et al., *Mastering*, p. 54.

8 Cathy Kaufman, 'What's in a Name? Some Thoughts on the Origin, Evolution, and Sad Demise of Béchamel Sauce', in *Milk: Beyond the Dairy*, ed. Harlan Walker (London, 2000), p. 198.

9 Christopher Grocock and Sally Grainger, eds, *Apicius: A Critical Edition* (London, 2006), recipe 8.6.6.

10 Marie-Antonin Carême, 'Traité des grandes sauces', *L'Art de la cuisine française au XIXe siècle* (Paris, 1833), vol. III, p. 3.

11 Pitte, *Gastronomie*, p. 130.

12 Hervé This, *Kitchen Mysteries*, trans. Jody Gladding (New York, 2007), p. 119.

13 Jean-Pierre Poulain and Edmond Neirinck, *Histoire de la cuisine et des cuisiniers*, 5th edn (Paris, 2004), p. 123.

14 Stephen Mennell, *All Manners of Food: Eating and Taste in England and France from the Middle Ages to the Present* (Chicago, IL, 1996), p. 239.

15 François Rabelais, *Le Quart-livre* (Paris, 1552), p. 164.

16 Eneas Sweetland Dallas, *Kettner's Book of the Table* (London, 1877), p. 5.

17 Alexandre Dumas, père, *Le Comte de Monte Cristo* [1846], ed. J. H. Bornecque (Paris, 1956), p. 739.

18 Louis Marin, *Food for Thought*, trans. Mette Hjort (Baltimore, MD, 1989), pp. 143–5.

19 Claude Fischler, *L'homnivore* (Paris, 1990), p. 264.

20 Gabriel Meurier, *Trésor de sentences dorées, dicts proverbes, et dictons communs* (Paris, 1581), p. 213.

21 Jean-Anthelme Brillat-Savarin, *Physiologie du goût* [1826] (Paris, 1982), p. 345.

22 Elizabeth David, *Spices, Salt, and Aromatics in the English Kitchen* (Harmondsworth, 1970), p. 75.

4 Gravy: Sauce for Meat, Sauce for Pasta

1 'Grain', 'Grané' and 'Gravé', *Dictionnaire du moyen français* (DMF 2012), ATILF – CNRS & Université de Lorraine, www.atilf.fr/dmf, accessed 26 September 2012.

2 Colin Spencer, *British Food: An Extraordinary Thousand Years of History* (New York, 2003), p. 106 .

3 William Kitchiner, *The Cook's Oracle* (London, 1817), p. 272; Kitchiner, *The Cook's Oracle* (Boston, 1822), p. 261.

4 Kitchiner, *The Cook's Oracle* (Boston, 1822), p. 260. Emphasis in original.

5 Susannah Carter, *The Frugal Housewife* (London, 1765), pp. 23–5.

6 Spencer, *British Food*, p. 276.

7 Mary Douglas and Michael Nicod, 'Taking the Biscuit: The Structure of British Meals', *New Society*, XXX/637 (December 1974), pp. 744–7.

8 Ibid., p. 746.

9 Ibid.

10 Massimo Montanari, *Food is Culture* [*Cibo come cultura*], trans. Albert Sonnenfeld (New York, 2006), p. 111.

11 George Allen McCue, 'The History of the Use of the Tomato: An Annotated Bibliography', *Annals of the Missouri Botanical Garden*, XXXIX/4 (1952), pp. 289–348.

12 Jeffrey M. Pilcher, *Que vivan los tamales! Food and the Making of Mexican Identity* (Albuquerque, NM, 1998), p. 50.

13 Rudolf Grewe, 'The Arrival of the Tomato in Spain and Italy: Early Recipes', *Journal of Gastronomy*, 3 (1987), p. 77.

14 Alberto Capatti and Massimo Montanari, *Italian Cuisine: A Cultural History*, trans. Aine O'Healy (New York, 2003), p. 55.

15 '. . . per indicare che i pomodori entrano per tutto'. Pellegrino Artusi, *La scienza in cucina e l'arte di mangiar bene* [1891] (Rome, 1983), p. 91.

16 Marcella Hazan, *The Classic Italian Cook Book* (New York, 1980), p. 28.

17 Silvano Serventi and Françoise Sabban, *Pasta: The Story of a Universal Food*, trans. Antony Shugaar (New York, 2002), pp. 263–4.

18 Franco La Cecla, *La pasta e la pizza* (Bologna, 1998), p. 77.

19 'Ragù', *Oxford Companion to Italian Food*, ed. Gillian Riley (Oxford, 2007), p. 433.

20 Marcella Hazan, *Essentials of Classic Italian Cooking* (New York, 1995), p. 150.

21 Donna R. Gabaccia, *We Are What We Eat: Ethnic Food and the Making of Americans* (Cambridge, MA, 1998), p. 151.

5 Odd Sauces

1 Marie-Antonin Carême, *Le Cuisinier parisien* (Paris, 1828), p. 24.

2 Menon, *Les Soupers de la cour* (Paris, 1755), vol. IV, pp. 314–15.

3 François Massialot, *Le Cuisinier royal et bourgeois* [1693], 2nd edn (Paris 1705), p. 224.

4 'Hershey's Syrup', Hershey Community Archives, www.hersheyarchives.org, accessed 1 November 2012.

5 'What Is In the Sauce That Is In the Big Mac?', http://yourquestions.mcdonalds.ca, posted 23 June 2012.

6 Robert May, *The Accomplisht Cook* [1660], 5th edn (London, 1685), section 1, n.p.

7 Quentin R. Skrabec, *H. J. Heinz: A Biography* (Durham, NC, 2009), p. 50.

8 Eneas Sweetland Dallas, *Kettner's Book of the Table* (London, 1877), p. 455.

9 'Welsh Rabbit', in *An A–Z of Food and Drink*, ed. John Ayto (Oxford, 2012).

10 'Cookery', *Household Words*, ed. Charles Dickens, III/61 (24 June 1882), p. 155.

11 Nathan Myrhvold, *Modernist Cuisine* (Washington, DC, 2011), vol. IV, p. 226.

12 Hervé This, *Kitchen Mysteries*, trans. Jody Gladding (New York, 2007), p. 4.

6 Global Variations and National Identity

1 See Louis-Eustache Ude, *The Art of Cookery* (London, 1815); Menon, *La Cuisinière bourgeoise* (Paris, 1746); and William Kitchiner, *The Cook's Oracle* (London, 1817).

2 Eliza Acton, *Modern Cookery* (London, 1868), p. 105. For a detailed recipe for 'the national sauce' see also Mary Hooper, *Good Plain Cookery* (London, 1882), p. 45.

3 Elizabeth David, *Spices, Salt and Aromatics in the English Kitchen* (Harmondsworth, 1970), p. 13.

4 Jean-Robert Pitte, *Gastronomie française: Histoire et géographie d'une passion* (Paris, 1991), p. 43.

5 'Ketchup a Vegetable in School Lunch Plan', *Pittsburgh Press*, 13 September 1981; 'USDA Approves Salsa as Vegetable', *Telegraph-Herald* (Iowa), 1 July 1998.

6 Colin Spencer, *British Food: An Extraordinary Thousand Years of History* (New York, 2003), p. 273.

7 'Cette sauce est bonne pour masquer des entrées qui n'ont pas bonne mine.' Menon, *La Cuisinière bourgeoise*, p. 154. The sauce ingredients are hard-boiled egg yolks, anchovies, capers, bouillon and *beurre manié*.

8 Eneas Sweetland Dallas, *Kettner's Book of the Table* (London, 1877), p. 2. On the subject of melted butter sauce, Dallas concedes, 'It is best to accept as a compliment the name which was meant as a reproach, and to call it the English Sauce', p. 301.

9 Louis, Saulnier, *Repertoire de la cuisine,* trans. E. Brunet (London, 1976), p. vii.

10 '. . . dans une science qui se vante d'être si éminemment française'. A. Tavenet, *Annuaire de la cuisine transcendante* (Paris, 1874), p. 45.

11 Jean-Louis Flandrin and Massimo Montanari, 'Conclusion: Today and Tomorrow', in *Food: A Culinary History*, ed. Albert Sonnenfeld (New York, 1999), p. 551.

12 'Per esempio [la pastasciutta] contrasta collo spirito vivace e coll'anima appassionata generosa intuitiva dei napoletani.' Filippo Marinetti, *Cucina futurista* (Milan, 1932), p. 28.

Select Bibliography

Capatti, Alberto, and Massimo Montanari, *Italian Cuisine:
   A Cultural History,* trans. Aine O'Healy (New York, 2003)
Child, Julia, Simone Beck and Louisette Bertholle, *Mastering
   the Art of French Cooking*, 2nd edn (New York, 1970)
Curtis, Robert, *Garum and Salsamenta* (New York, 1991)
David, Elizabeth, *Spices, Salt and Aromatics in the English Kitchen*
   (Harmondsworth, 1970)
Diat, Louis, *Sauces, French and Famous* (New York, 1951)
Flandrin, Jean-Louis, Massimo Montanari and Albert
   Sonnenfeld, *Food: A Culinary History from Antiquity to the
   Present* (New York, 1999)
Grocock, Christopher, and Sally Grainger, eds, *Apicius:
   A Critical Edition* (London, 2006)
Huang, H. T., and Joseph Needham, *Science and Civilization
   in China*, vol. vi, part 5 of *Fermentations and Food Science*
   (Cambridge, 2000)
Larousse gastronomique (Paris, 2000)
Mennell, Stephen, *All Manners of Food: Eating and Taste in England
   and France from the Middle Ages to the Present* (Chicago, il, 1996)
Myhrvold, Nathan, *Modernist Cuisine* (Washington, dc, 2011)
Peterson, James, *Sauces*, 3rd edn (Hoboken, nj, 2008)
Pilcher, Jeffrey M., *Que vivan los tamales! Food and the Making of
   Mexican Identity* (Albuquerque, nm, 1998)
Pitte, Jean-Robert, *French Gastronomy: The History and Geography of
   a Passion*, trans. Jody Gladding (New York, 2002)

Poulain, Jean-Pierre, and Edmond Neirinck, *Histoire de la cuisine et des cuisiniers*, 5th edn (Paris, 2004)

Riley, Gillian, ed., *Oxford Companion to Italian Food* (Oxford, 2007)

Serventi, Silvano, and Françoise Sabban, *Pasta: The Story of A Universal Food*, trans. Antony Shugaar (New York, 2002)

Smith, Andrew, ed., *Oxford Companion to American Food and Drink* (Oxford, 2007)

—, *Pure Ketchup: A History of America's National Condiment* (Columbia, SC, 1996)

Spencer, Colin, *British Food: An Extraordinary Thousand Years of History* (New York, 2003)

Steinkraus, Keith, ed., *Industrialization of Indigenous Fermented Foods*, 2nd edn (New York, 2004)

This, Hervé, *Kitchen Mysteries: Revealing the Science of Cooking*, trans. Jody Gladding (New York, 2007)

Toussaint-Samat, Maguelonne, *A History of Food*, trans. Anthea Bell (Chichester, 2009)

Willan, Anne, *Great Cooks and their Recipes* (New York, 1977)

Websites and Associations

Sauce History

Academia Barilla Gastronomic Library
www.academiabarilla.com/gastronomic-library

Food Timeline: Sauces and Dips
www.foodtimeline.org/foodsauces

Heinz History Center
www.heinzhistorycenter.org

Soy Info Center
www.soyinfocenter.com

Sauce Enthusiasts

Association for Dressings and Sauces
www.dressings-sauces.org

Béarnaise: Recipes, History, and More!
www.bearnaise.org

Bon Appétit Sauce Recipes
www.bonappetit.com/ideas/sauce-recipes

Campaign for Real Gravy
www.realgravy.co.uk

Ketchup: Let's Get It On
http://ketchup.com

Peppers and More: A Foodies Guide to Fire, Spice, and Flavor
http://peppersandmore.com

PopSugar Food: National Sauce Month
www.yumsugar.com/latest/National-Sauce-Month

Acknowledgements

I am grateful to Bard College at Simon's Rock for granting me a semester-long sabbatical leave in the fall of 2012 that made writing this book possible. Grants from the Faculty Development Fund allowed me to participate in a number of conferences, including the University of Texas at San Antonio Food Representation conference in 2010, where I first presented a paper on sauces in French literature. Dean Anne O'Dwyer has my sincere thanks for her enthusiasm for this project and her patience with my absence. My colleagues in the Division of Language and Literature helpfully provided coverage for my courses and their interest in my research, especially Gabriel Asfar, has been a constant source of encouragement. The library staff at Simon's Rock supplied invaluable interlibrary loan service and research support, and I am fortunate to have had access to the collections of the Central and Western Massachusetts Library Consortium and the Williams College Library. Special thanks go to Zachary Nowak and Elgin Eckert for organizing the Umbra Institute Italian Food Conference in June 2012, which gave me another outlet for my Italian sauce research and connected me to new colleagues in food studies. I am indebted to Janet Okoben for her expert editing of a number of chapters late in the game, and thanks go to Nell McCabe for her suggestions on the French and Italian chapters. Finally, my sons Noah and Ethan gave me technical and moral support and endured many sauce tales at the dinner table over the course of this project. I promise that we can talk about something else now.

Permissions

Photo Acknowledgements

The author and the publishers wish to express their thanks to the below sources of illustrative material and /or permission to reproduce it.

The Art Archive at Art Resource, New York: p. 15 (NGS Image Collection); Art Resource, New York: p. 37 (V&A Images); Courtesy Daniel Bexfield, Bexfield Antiques, www.bexfield.co.uk: p. 80; Biblioteca Gastronomica Academia Barilla (Collection of Livio Cerini de Castegnate): p. 125; Bibliothèque Nationale de France: pp. 60, 65; © Trustees of the British Museum, London: pp. 14, 17, 21, 75, 77; Peter Carney: p. 30; DJM: p. 45; Detre Library and Archives, Sen. John Heinz History Center, Pittsburgh, Pennsylvania: p. 106; Paul Downey: p. 8; ElinorD: p. 114; © Grace's Guide: pp. 10, 39, 82; iStock: p. 132 (Junghee Choi); Joadl: p. 101; Lara Kastner: p. 116; © Kikkoman Corporation: p. 18; © Kraft Foods: p. 35; © McDonald's Canada: p. 103; Ourren: p. 36; © Ragú Foods: p. 95; Shutterstock: pp. 33 (bonchan), 46 (Simon van den Berg), 57 (Dustin Dennis), 64 (Piyato), 71 (Patty Orly), 85 (Stills Photography), 91 (Shebeko), 104 (Otokimus), 111 (jreika), 113 (Monkey Business Images), 117 (Moving Moment), 121 (Ildi Papp), 122 (alisafarov), 126 (Africa Studio), 128 (bonchan), 130 (Martin Turzak); Rainer Zenz: p. 42.

Index

italic numbers refer to illustrations; **bold** to recipes